The Eyes of Raymond Hu

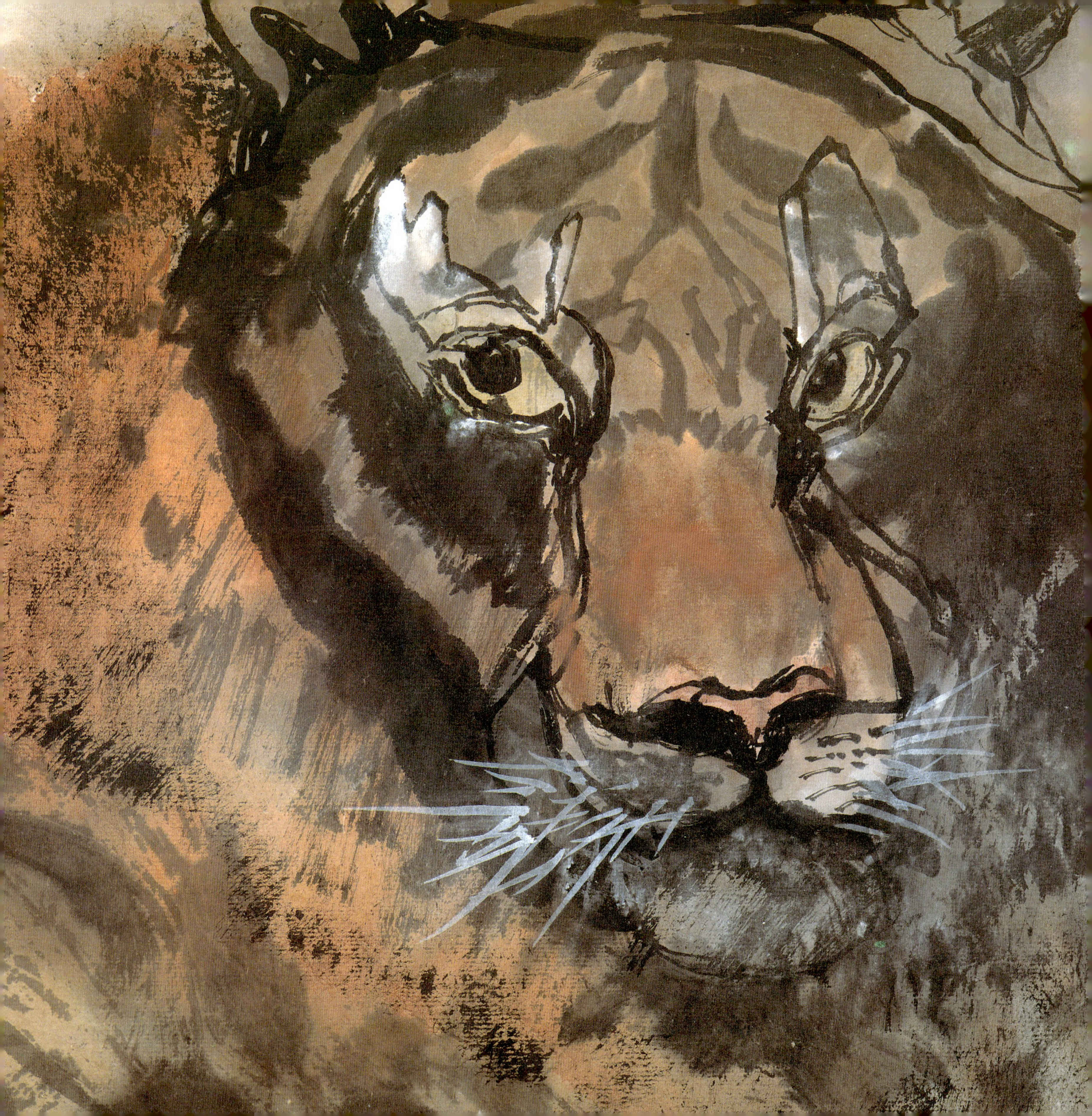

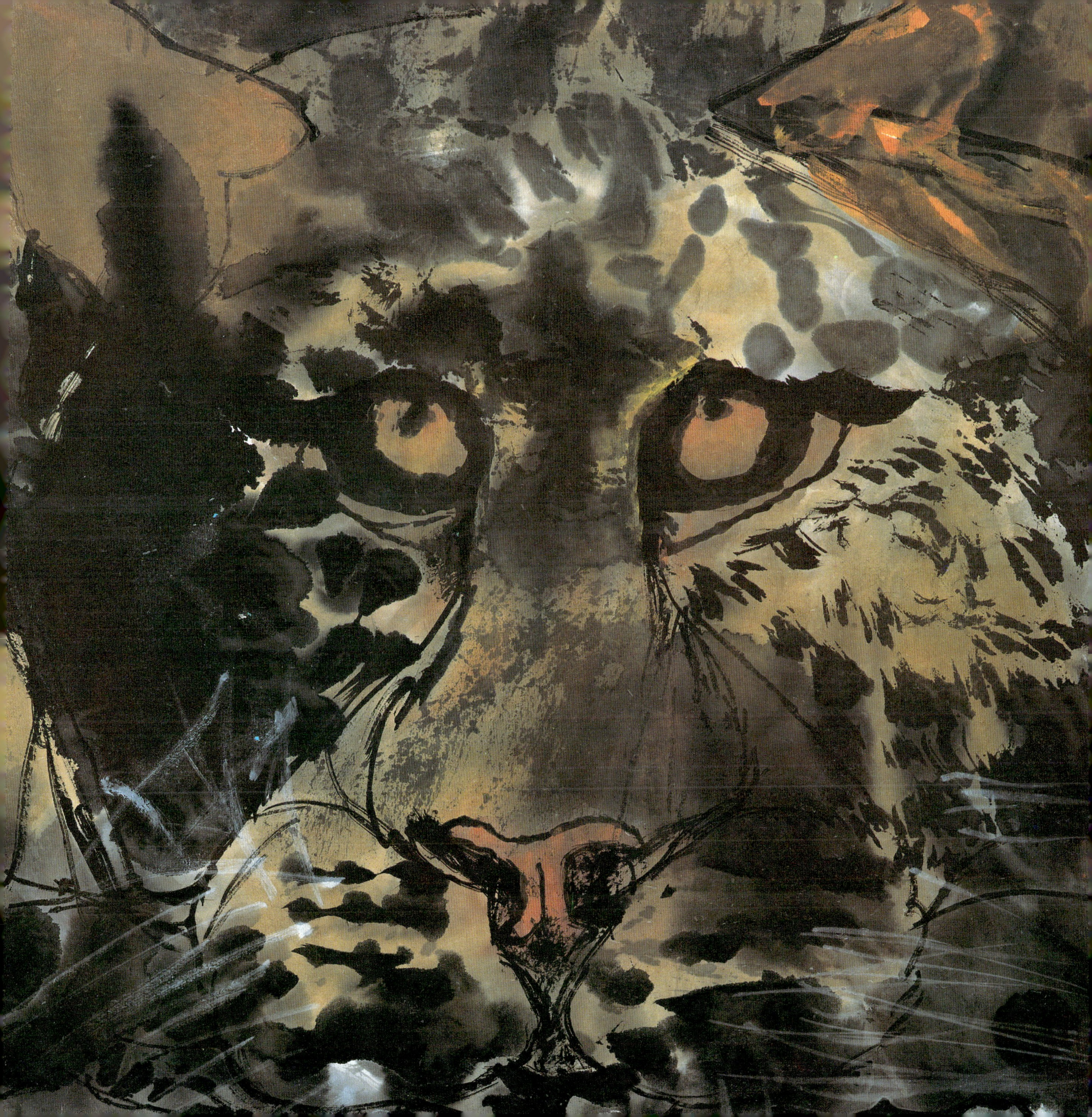

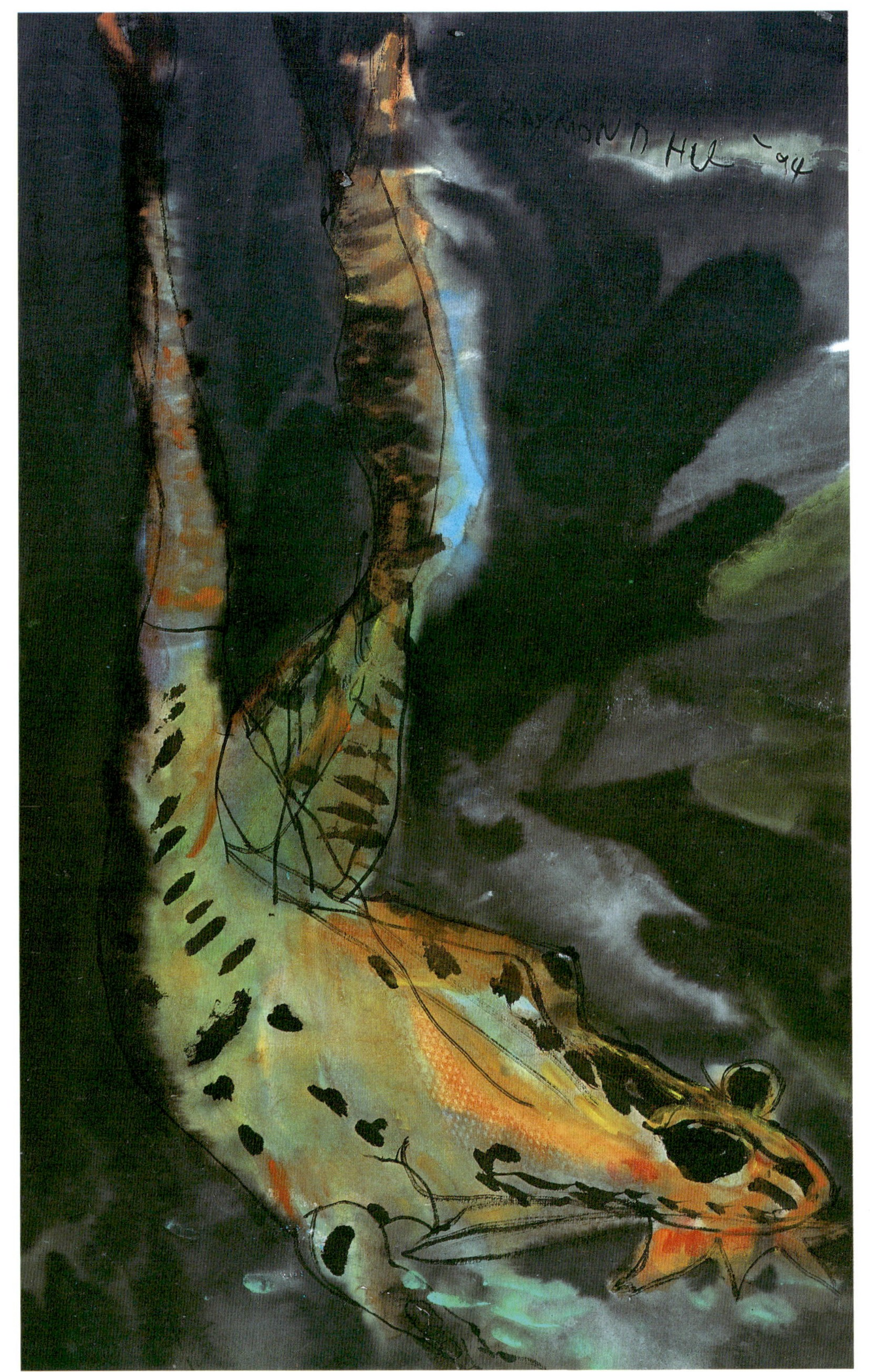

RAYMOND HU '94

The Eyes of Raymond Hu

Brush Paintings by Raymond Hu
Foreword by So Kam Lee
Introduction by Lampo Leong

安
宇
心
象

Art Media Resources, Ltd
Chicago, USA

安宇心象

繪畫：胡安宇

序言：吳素琴

評論：梁藍波

攝影：藍　波

設計：藍　波

出版：美國藝術資源

版次：1996年11月第一版

版權所有，不得翻印

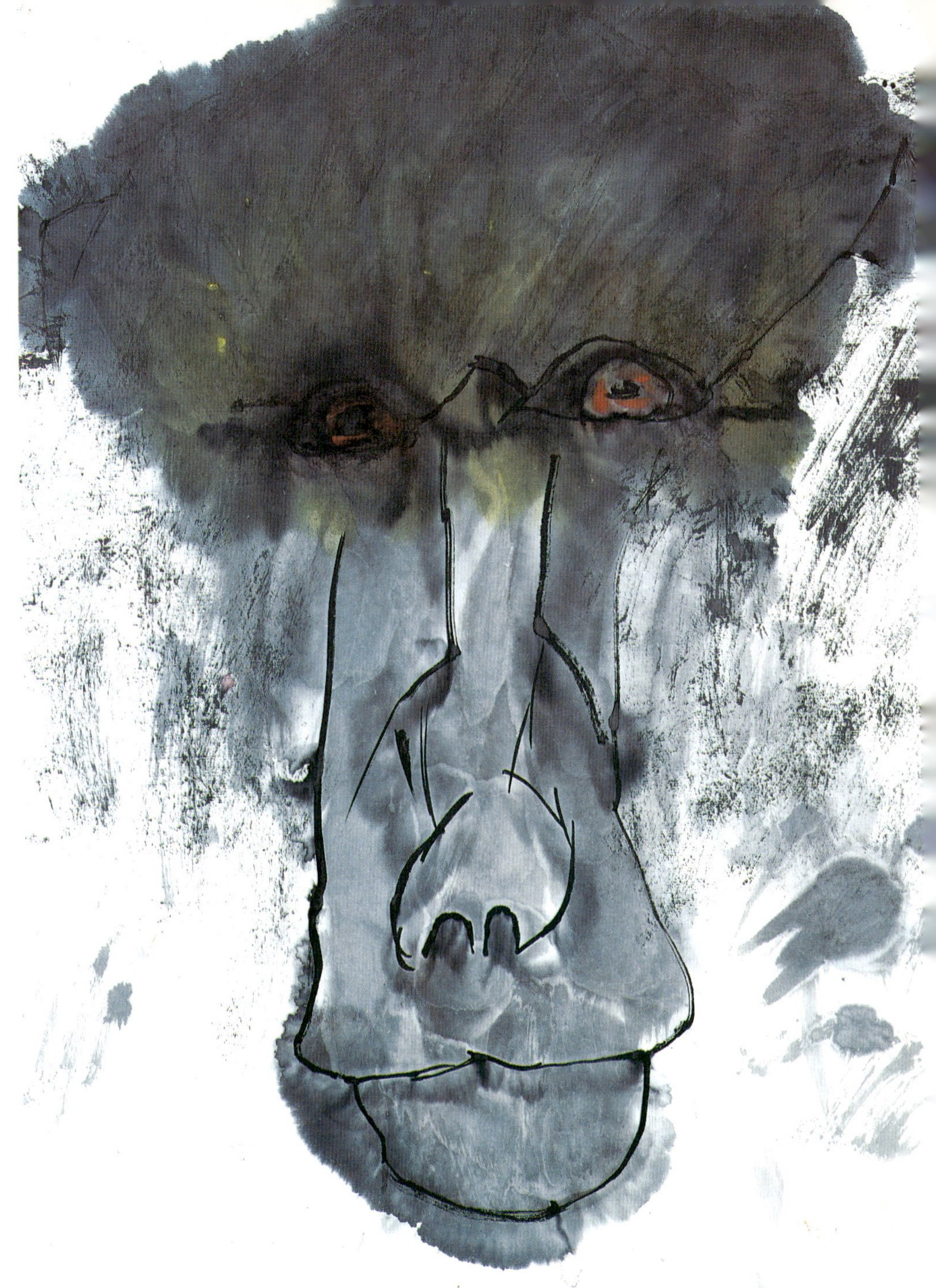

The Eyes of Raymond Hu
Brush Paintings by Raymond Hu
Foreword by So Kam Lee
Introduction by Lampo Leong

Designer: Lanbo Liang
Photographer: Lanbo Liang

Publisher: Art Media Resources, Ltd.
　　　　　　Chicago, USA
Distributed by Brushstrokes
　　　　　PO Box 722
　　　　　Alamo, CA 94507-0722 USA
　　　　　Fax: 510-820-3398

ISBN 1-878529-20-X
US $ 25.00

Front cover: *Nocturnal Glow* (Detail), 1996 《紅光》
Front endsheets: *Regal Lion* (Detail), 1995 《獅子王》
　　　　　　　　Gazing Leopard (Detail), 1995 《凝眸》
Title page: *Diving Frog*, 1994 《水中青蛙》
This page: *The Yellow Baboon*, 1994 《狒狒》
Back endsheets: *Autumn Reflection* (Detail), 1996 《秋色》
　　　　　　　　Red-faced Monkey (Detail), 1996 《紅色的投影》
Back cover: *Soaring Spoonbill*, 1996 　《翱翔》

目錄

CONTENTS

Foreword: The Paintings of Raymond Hu

So Kam Lee

The paintings of Raymond Hu are striking in that they confront their viewers with thoughtful and provocative expressions. It is remarkable that such a young artist is able to handle the difficult media of Chinese brush, ink, and paper. These works are even more extraordinary given Raymond Hu's restricted motor skills due to Down Syndrome. More importantly, the key element that sets Raymond's paintings apart from the art work of other nineteen-year-olds, or even older and more mature artists, is how he has captured the spirit of his subjects and imbued them with some measure of humanity. For Raymond, these works are portraits of animals he obviously cares for and identifies with.

Raymond Hu likes to paint animals and birds. He uses photographs from wildlife magazines as models. Starting with the eyes, Hu sketches out the basic form of his subject in ink, then finishes it with applications of ink and color washes. The portraits are close-up views of the animals, with emphasis on the face and eyes. Although Hu takes great care in capturing the distinctive physical features of the animals, and one can easily recognize the specific species, they are not realistic depictions. In fact, some are almost abstract. These creatures stare out with expressions ranging from playfulness to weariness, from great agitation to intense sadness. Their soulful gaze draws and intrigues the audience. Raymond paints as if he understands and comprehends their emotions and predicaments. His sensitivity and affinity for his subject are clearly evident.

In *Happy Elephant* and *Franklin's Cat*, works from 1993, the subjects express a joyful and mischievous quality that is bright and very appealing. The open mouth and uplifted trunk of the elephant convey a great sense of elation. *Franklin's Cat*, with its coyly twisted form, reflects the playful nature of this well-loved pet.

The Laughing Ostrich on the other hand seems to be uttering the shrieking cry of someone being provoked. The feeling of vigor and excitement is depicted through a concentration on the head, especially the wide opened mouth, which is rendered with sharp and angular lines. The intense and highly diffused applications of ink for the body give a feeling of motion and great vitality.

A totally different emotion is expressed in *Mournful Tiger*. The sagging lines and twisted form intensify the sentiment of sadness and complete dejection. In a more recent work, *Old Yeller,* one can recognize a tired and weary soul whose dimmed eyes still sparkle with wisdom and experience. The dull shades of ink and color give the appearance of advanced age.

The animals that interest the artist most are carnivores and those endangered because of man's destructive actions. Hu is adamant about the protection of the environment, the need for recycling, and the prevention of further pollution. He feels that man is responsible for disrupting the food chain of the animals. In his works, Hu expresses sympathy for both man and animals and an understanding of how one is intrinsically linked to the other.

So Kam Lee is a former curator of the Asian Art Museum in San Francisco who specializes in modern Chinese painting.

Raymond Hu started painting in 1990. His parents, impressed by a brush painting by Lampo Leong, a San Francisco Bay Area artist, began their lessons with this local master. At first Raymond and his younger brother passively observed the process. However, after some prompting, both joined, making it a family activity. At first, the process was slow and difficult for Raymond, given his physical limitations. With time and encouragement from his parents and teacher, but most of all through his own perseverance, Raymond finally found a vehicle for his feelings and creativity in painting animals. They serve as his voice that speaks passionately and eloquently for their creator.

Although Raymond Hu has been painting for a relatively short time, his works have gone through several distinctive stages. Paintings from 1993 are characterized by bright, cheerful colors. The images are lively and highly animated. There is a general sentiment of joy and youthful innocence. Works from 1995 are more serious in expression. There are more repeated applications of ink and colors, giving the figures a richer and more substantial quality. 1996 marks a new stage in the art of Raymond Hu. His lines are more decisive and sophisticated, colors more earthy and subtle. The emotions are more complex and intriguing.

Raymond Hu's art is a product of his talent and circumstance. His animal portraits express a vision that is original and very personal. The vitality of his work corresponds to an intensity of feelings that is well served by his use of bold, uncompromising strokes and vibrant colors. His animals look out with soulful eyes that beckon the viewer to ponder and reflect. He has infused his animal portraits with his own spirit, making them expressions of his inner world, his feelings and dreams.

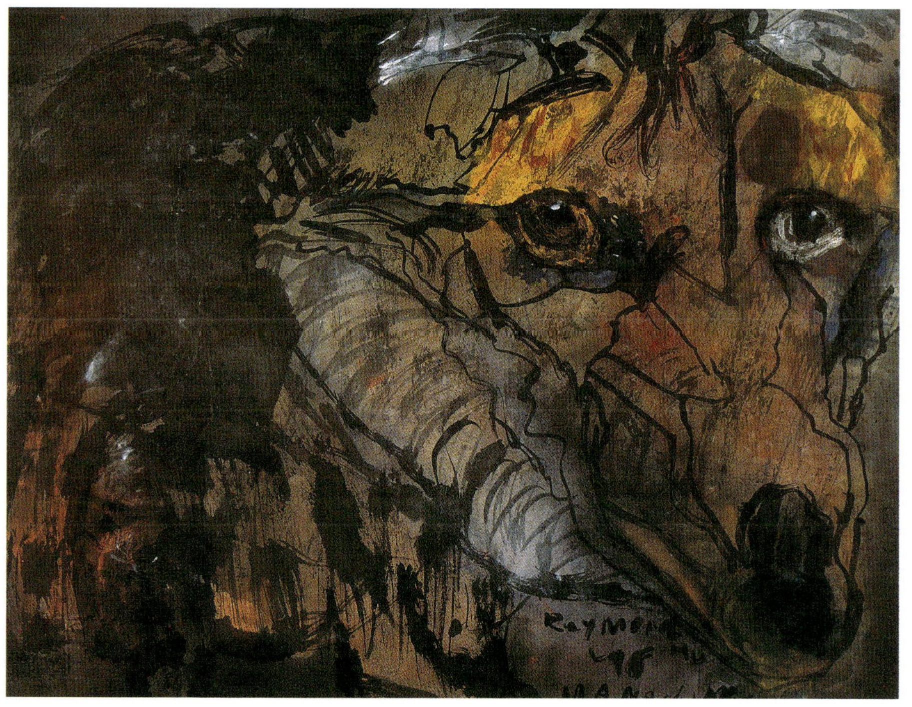

9 • SOULFUL EYES, Chinese Ink & Watercolor on Rice-paper, 13.5 x 18 inches (34 x 46 cm), 1996 《凝神》彩墨設色紙本

安 宇 心 象　　　梁藍波

世上有兩種藝術家，一種是開放型，通過後天的多方學習去認識事物從而找尋自我。人生的過程由外及裡，從掌握技巧著手漸漸達到精神的表現。這種人較易學習新的東西，能做到全面發展，但要做到獨特，達到高峰需時略長。另一種藝術家是封閉型，對一些事物有天生的敏感，往往通過自身的特殊直覺去感悟世界。從精神出發去尋找依附的形式和表達的技巧。這種人往往不易學到新的東西，不太全面，但卻會在某些方面有異常突出的表現。人生的過程重在發掘生命裡固有的、閃光的本體從而完善自我。這類人如果被恰當地引導極可能很快就進入角色。

顯然，胡安宇屬於後者，而且是這類人的典型代表。我在教畫的過程中亦對他重在引導，僅帶他入門，指個方向，讓他自己去探索、發揮。他對形象有特殊的感覺，對中國畫的媒材也有天生的操縱能力。在學畫的短短五、六年裡能夠很快觸及自己的靈魂，走過從具象邁向心象的路程。

安宇是個智障少年，患有先天性唐氏綜合症對他正常的學習帶來了很大的障礙。在父母嘔心瀝血的關懷下和老師的耐心栽培下，他不斷努力，克服了重重困難，終於完成了高中課程並升入大學。而且在某些課程上顯示出他獨特的才華，諸如歷史、地理等，他對日期、事件的細節有超乎常人的記憶力。他喜愛動物也對它們很有感情，很有研究。他作畫的題材以動物為主，形象來源於他收藏的動物雜誌中的照片。但他畫起來誇張變形、取捨明確，僅借助動物及動物的眼神去表露自我的心靈。

藝術作品無法擺脫作者的個性及其人生經歷。安宇源於對細節的獨特注意力，他比常人對動物觀察得更細，把畫畫得更深入，有如用放大鏡把細節放大到大於整體的程度。這種精微的細節與整體的錯位組合，顧此忘彼的取捨特點使他的動物肖像介乎寫實與抽象之間，介乎人與動物之間，將自我溶入到動物裡，使作品更貼近於他內心世界裡的、幻覺中的形象。

安宇這種大特寫式的表現手法使他畫的動物呼之欲出，眼睛炯炯有神。瞳孔、高光都表現精到，無論你從那個方向觀畫，眼睛都好像跟隨著你，與觀眾產生眼對眼的直接溝通。

安宇個性執著，對日程安排非常固執，不得變更。房間各物所放的位置也非常固定，不得隨便移動。這種執著使他的繪畫具有非常明確的意識，落筆肯定、線條凝重，意境絕不含糊。

在學畫的短短幾年裡，安宇的作品走過了幾個重要的階段。開始時因為他的生理條件，他比別的學生有更多更多的困難去掌握中國畫的筆墨技巧。畢竟，水彩墨汁在宣紙上的反應是非常的敏感：用墨的乾濕與濃淡，用筆的輕重與緩急，用心的專注與散漫，用神的肯定與遲疑，運氣的連貫與斷裂都能在落入宣紙上的墨痕裡一覽無遺。對任何一個學生來說都需要很多的訓練才能在宣紙毛筆中找到感覺，達到得心應手。

九三年起安宇開始能操控筆墨，駕御形象，畫出很好的作品。這個時期筆墨明快，色彩亮麗，形象生動，生機盎然。感情基調天真愉快，溢滿孩子般的幻想。

九五年的作品開始變得沉實內在。筆墨上除了勾線之外多了些皴擦，層次漸顯豐富，色彩走向含蓄。眼神中多了一份深邃與持重。

到了九六年，安宇的作品產生了一個非常重要的飛躍。他捨棄了表面的生動，而轉入內心情感的發掘，開始悟及自己的靈魂。感情更加收斂，深沉內在；線條更加繁密凝重，縱橫交錯；筆觸更加豐富多變，皴擦破染交織；墨韻濃淡有致，更顯出層次；形象扭曲誇張，細節與整體的錯位組合更為隨意；構圖更加充實飽滿，且富有張力；明暗對比強烈而更具戲劇性；色彩更加沉厚幽暗，濃鬱而富於觸感；眼睛更有神韻卻更為隱藏，就好像藏在靈魂背後，在幽暗中放發著靈光，散發出一種無法抗拒的感召力和攝人心魄的魅力。這些動物形象大大脫離了動物而變為安宇夢幻中的生靈，表現出一種居於幕後的、隱藏的，卻更為大度的、主宰者的浩然氣派。

安宇藝術的成功並不基於他的生理因素，但他獨特的生命本體和生活壓力強化了他的個性。這種像孩子般的直率與執著使他對世界下意識的直覺和他內心的情感得以不加修飾地、毫無保留地傾注在畫中的一筆一劃。藝術貴在真誠，只有肺腑之言才能感人肺腑。安宇看似天真爛熳的作品實質上蘊涵著莫大的渾厚與深刻。他用筆蘸著心血去畫，用他自己心靈的激蕩去啟動人類的感情世界，掀動著觀眾的心。有意無意之間，他已經觸及藝術的真諦。

丙子深秋於天涯山居

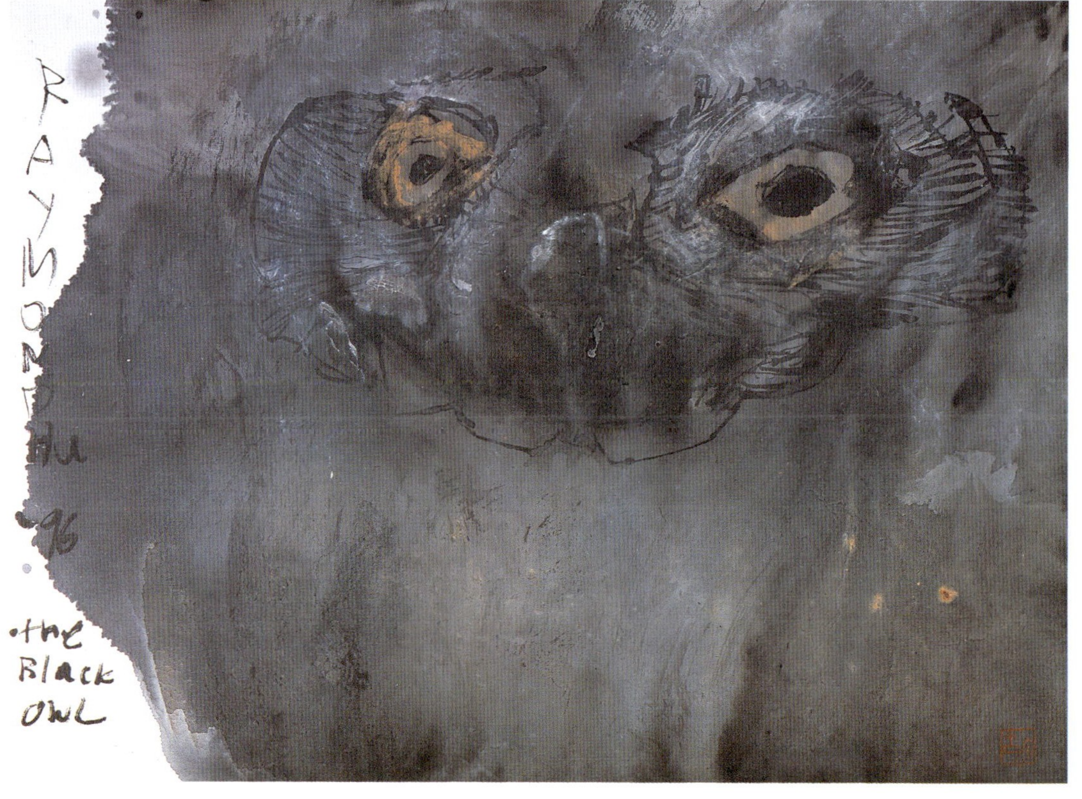

11 • THE BLACK OWL, Chinese Ink & Watercolor on Rice-paper, 13.5 x 18 inches (34 x 46 cm), 1996　《天外來客》紙本

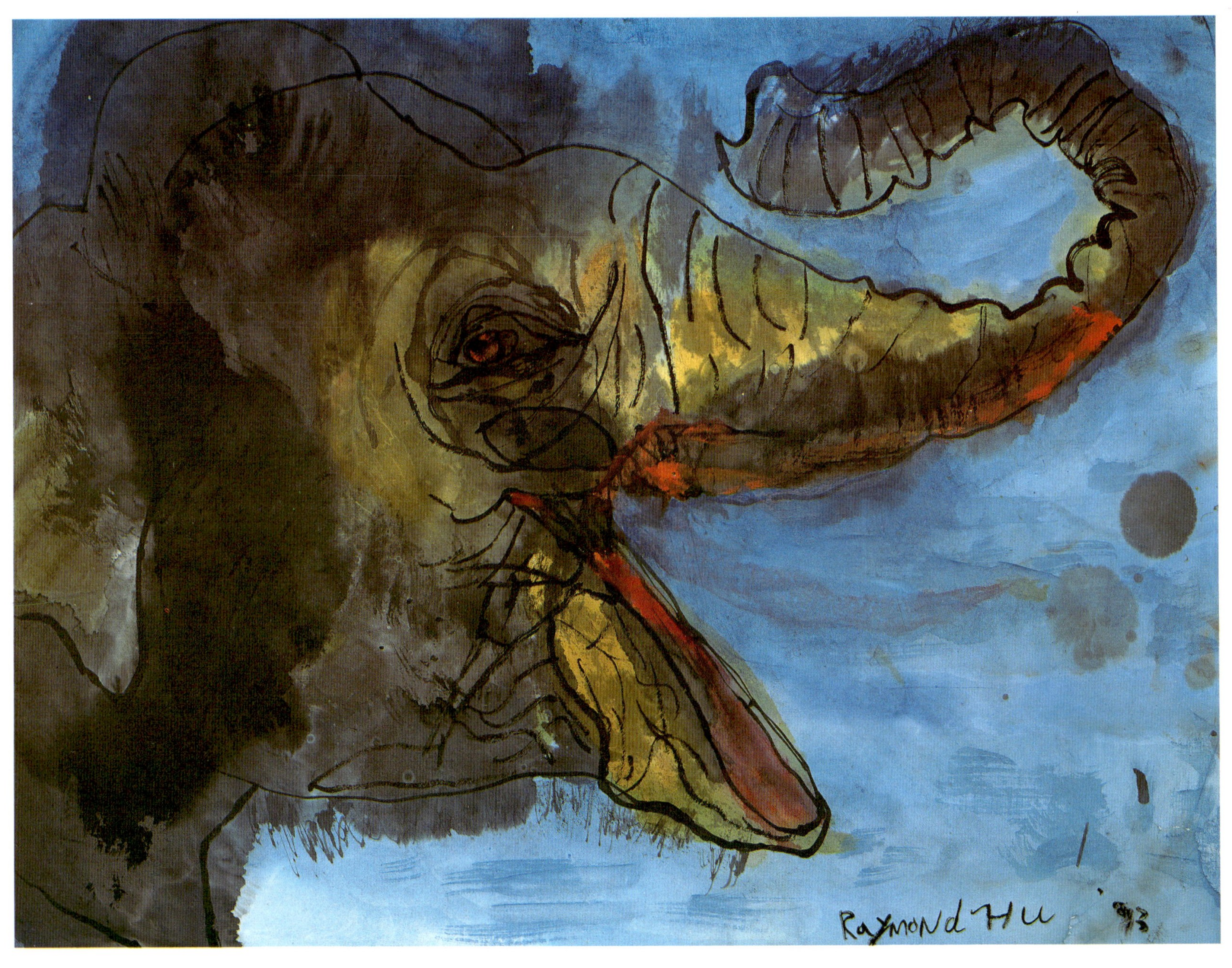

12 • THE HAPPY ELEPHANT, Chinese Ink & Watercolor on Rice-paper, 13.5 x 18 inches (34 x 46 cm), 1993 《大象》設色紙本

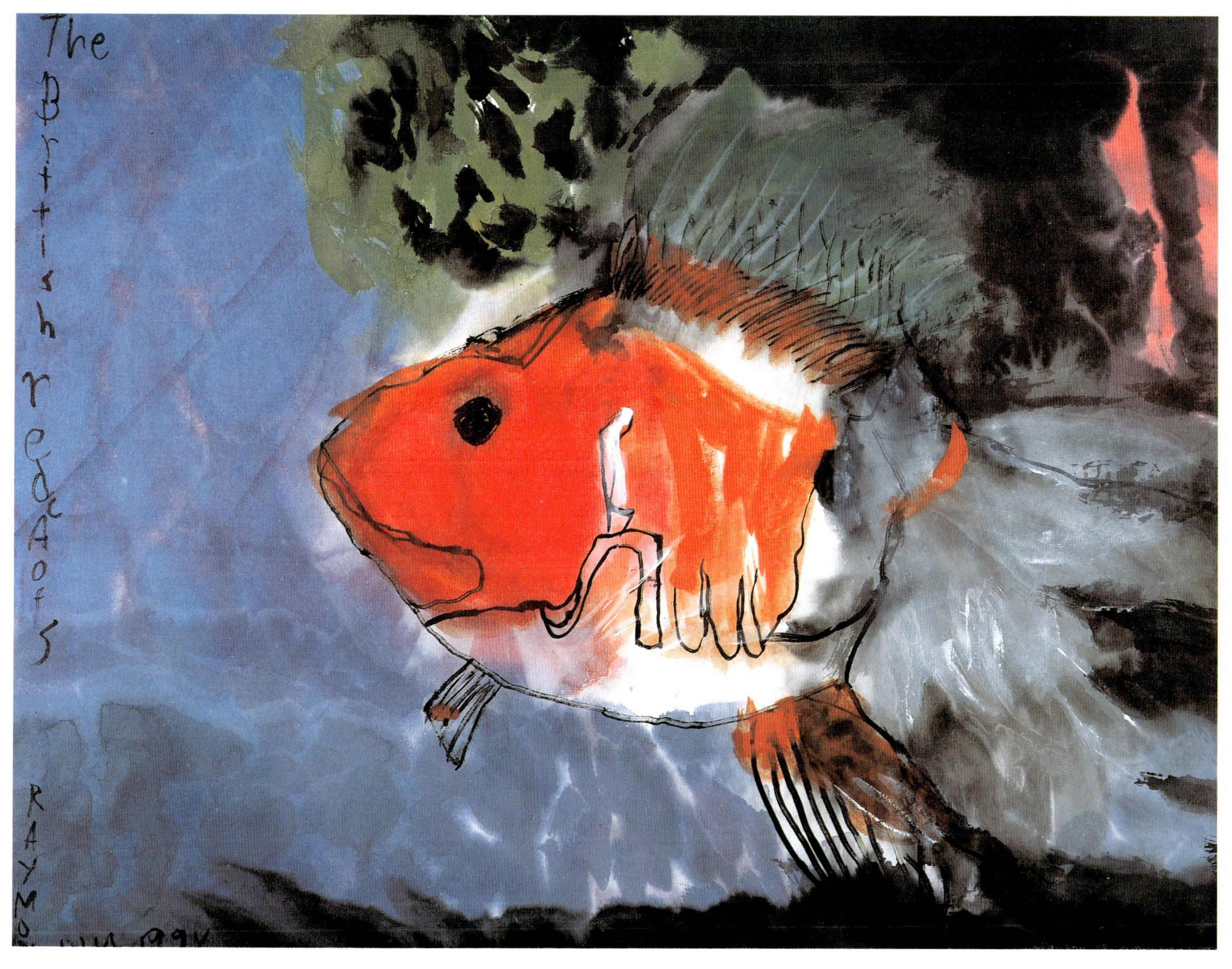

13 • THE BRITISH RED COATS, Chinese Ink & Watercolor on Rice-paper, 13.5 x 18 inches (34 x 46 cm), 1994 《紅裝》 紙本

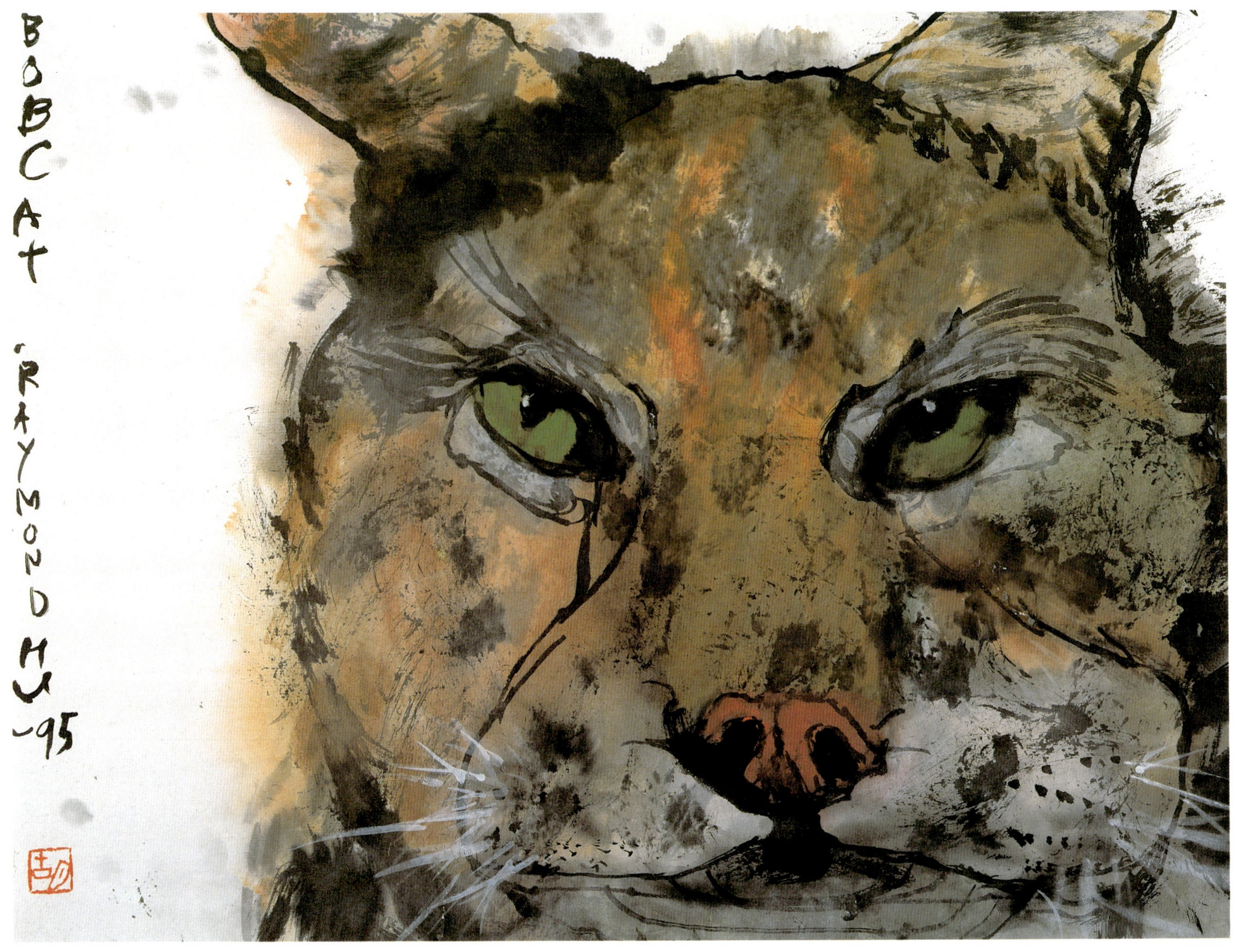

14 • BOBCAT, Chinese Ink & Watercolor on Rice-paper, 13.5 x 18 inches (34 x 46 cm), 1995 　　　《昂首遠矚》彩墨設色紙本

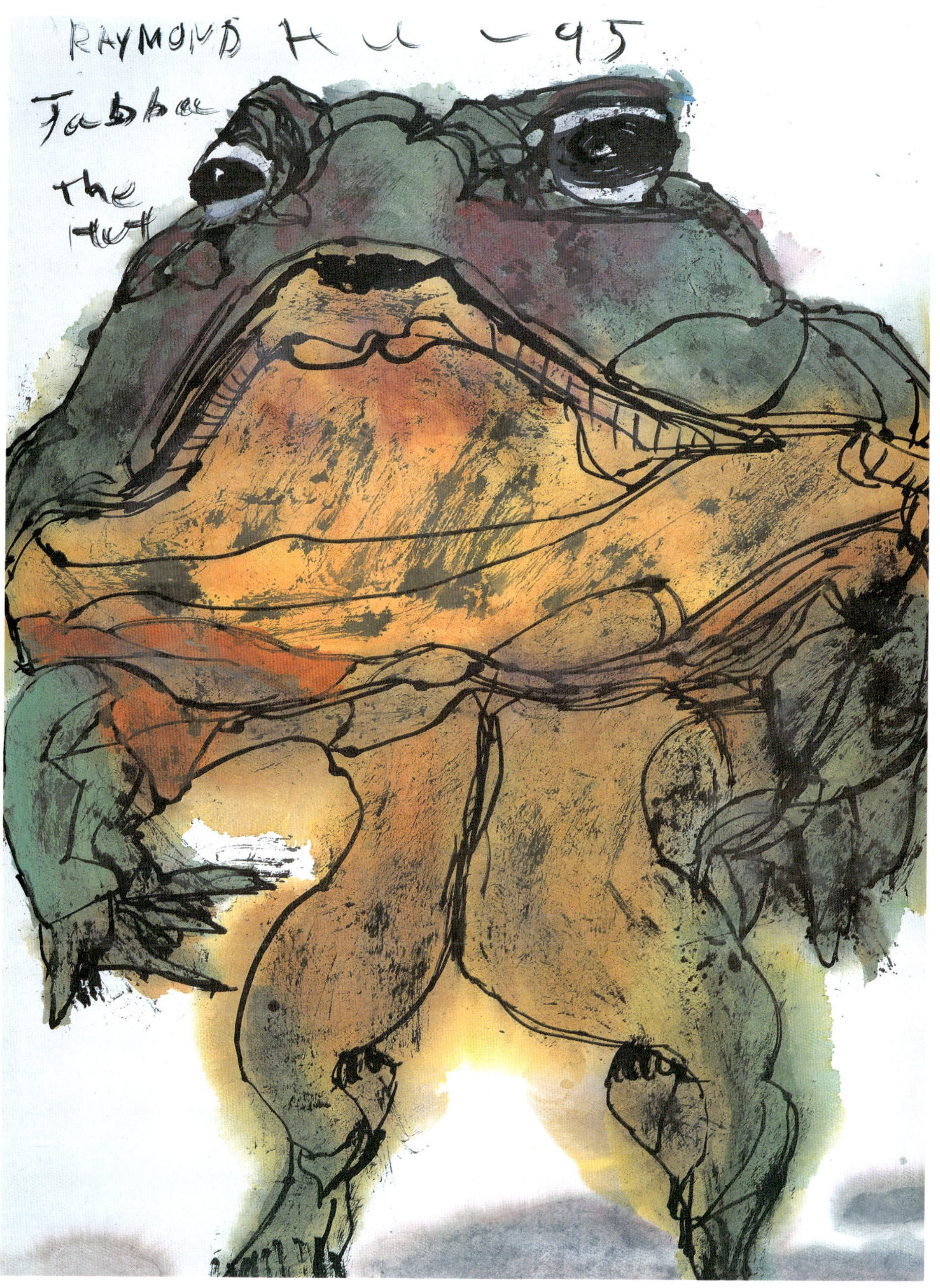

《聞歌起舞》設色紙本

• DANCING FROG, Chinese Ink & Watercolor on Rice-paper, 18 x 13.5 inches (46 x 34 cm), 1995

15

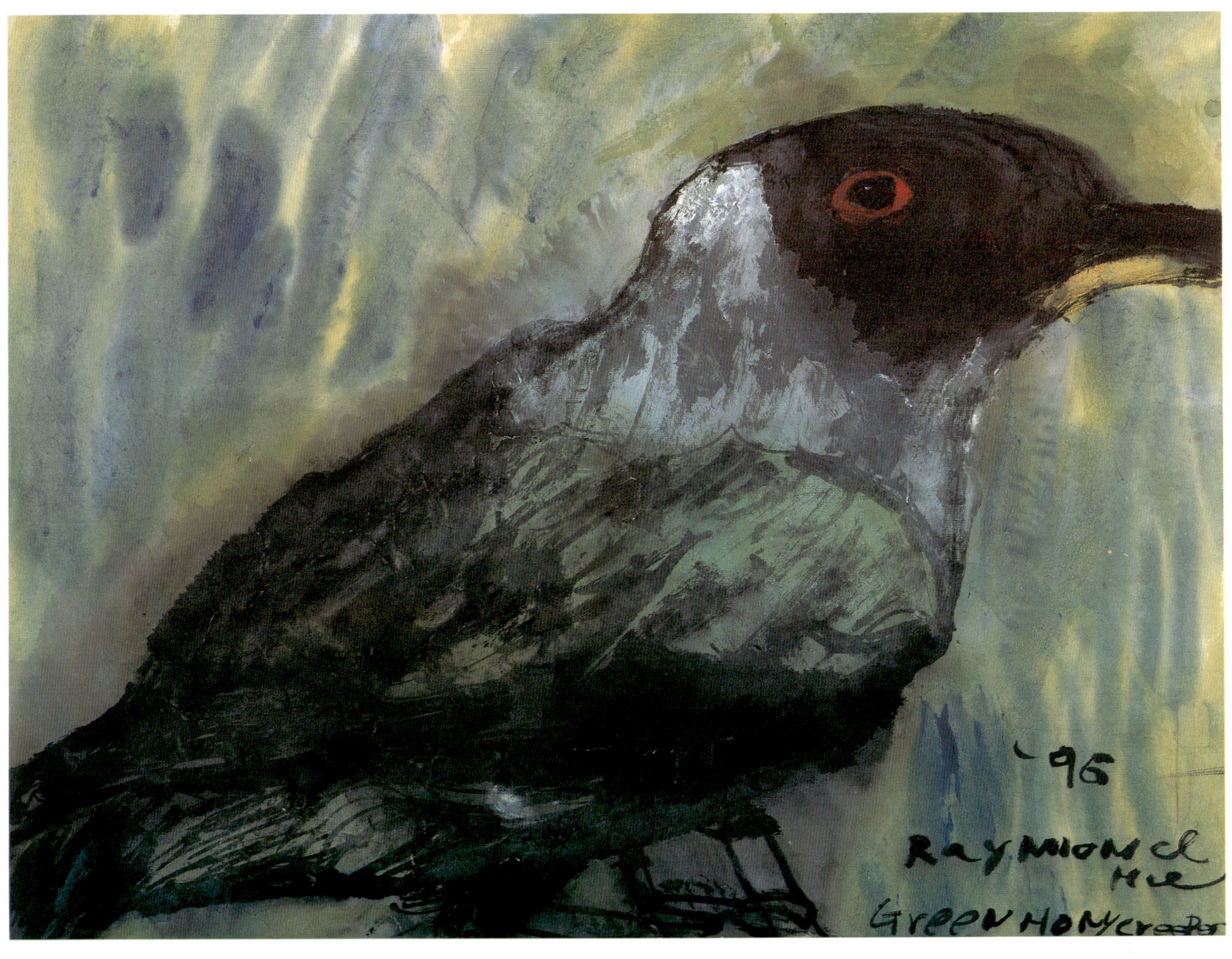

16 • GREEN HONEY CREEPER, Chinese Ink & Watercolor on Rice-paper, 13.5 x 18 inches (34 x 46 cm), 1996　《春雨瀟瀟》

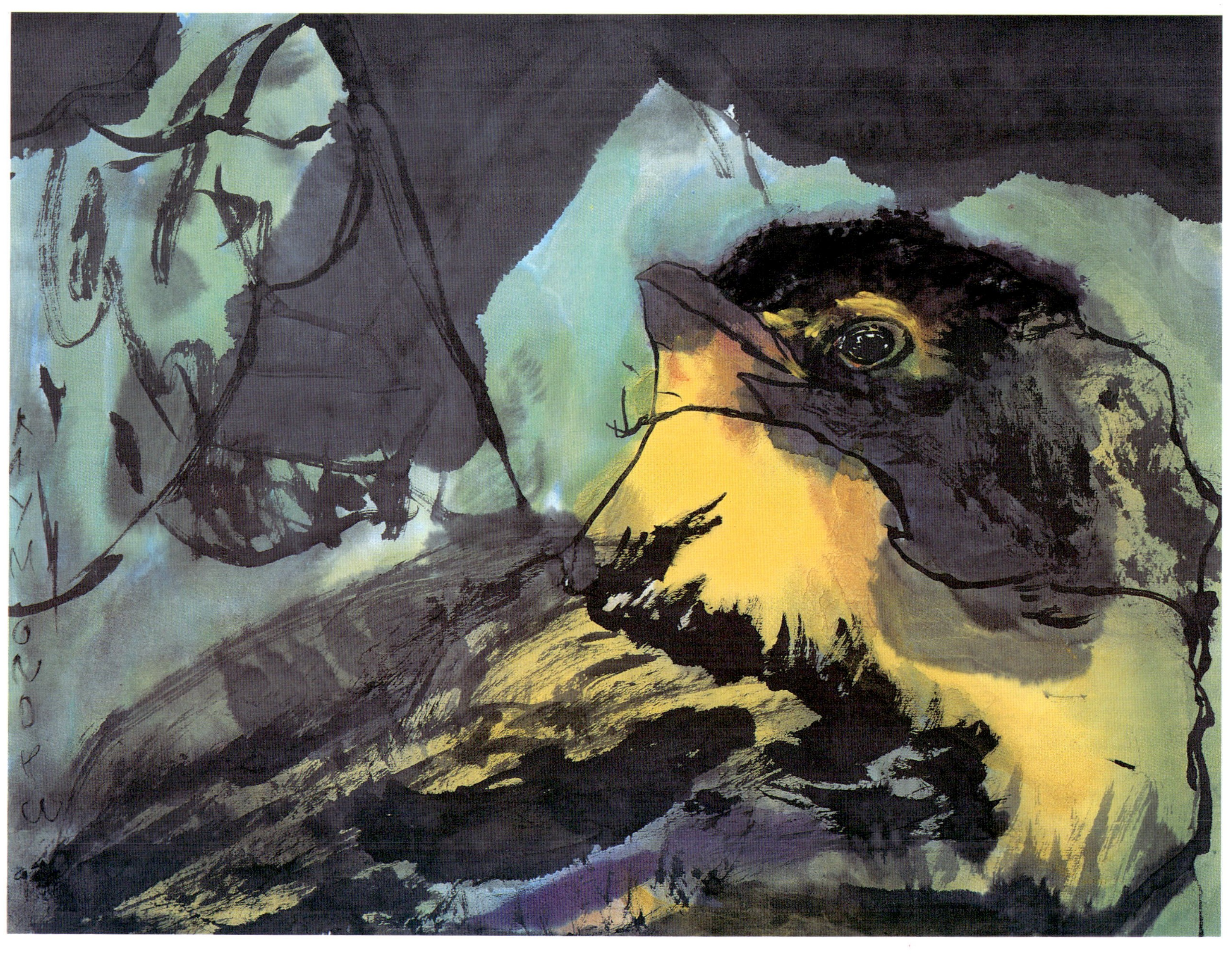

17 • SPRING RAIN, Chinese Ink & Watercolor on Rice-paper, 13.5 x 18 inches (34 x 46 cm), 1993　　《綠蔭》彩墨設色紙本

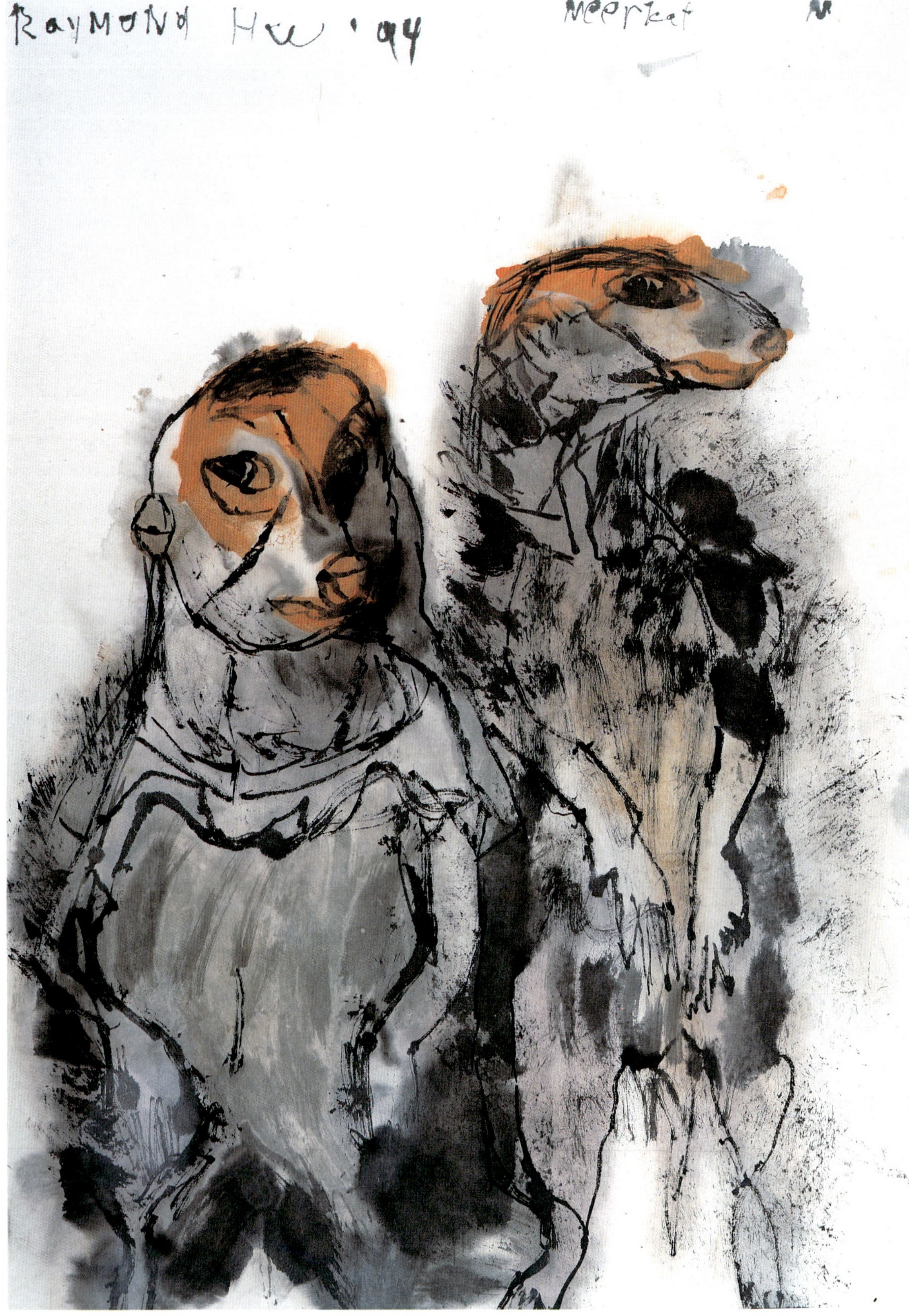

《兄弟倆》彩墨設色紙本

• BROTHERS, Chinese Ink & Watercolor on Rice-paper, 19 x 13.5 inches (48 x34 cm), 1994

18

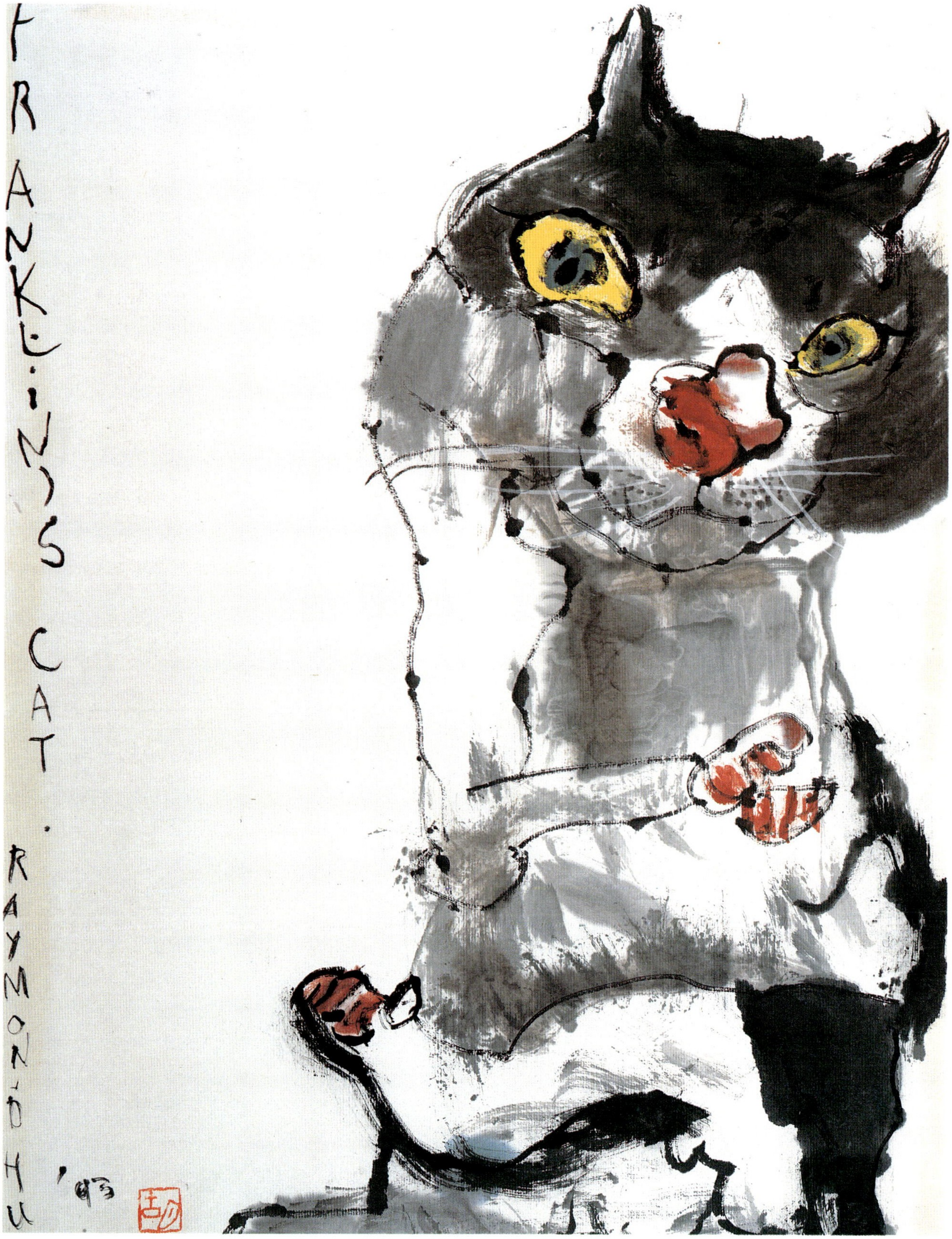

《戲貓》 彩墨設色紙本

• FRANKLIN'S CAT, Chinese Ink & Watercolor on Rice-paper, 18 x 13.5 inches (46 x 34 cm), 1993

19

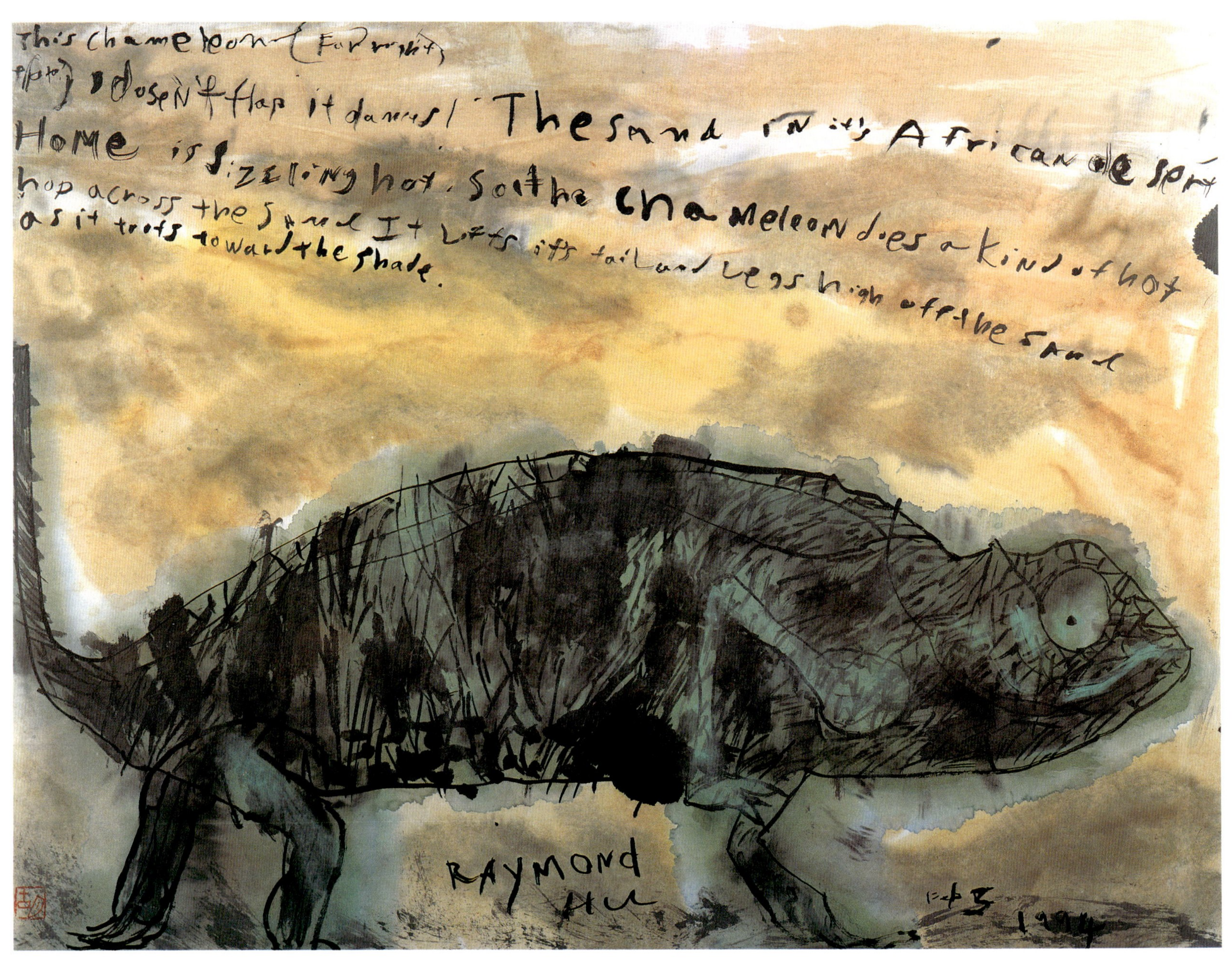

20 • HIP HOP ON THE SIZZLING SAND, Chinese Ink & Watercolor on Rice-paper, 18 x 24 inches, 1994　《沙漠嬌陽》紙本

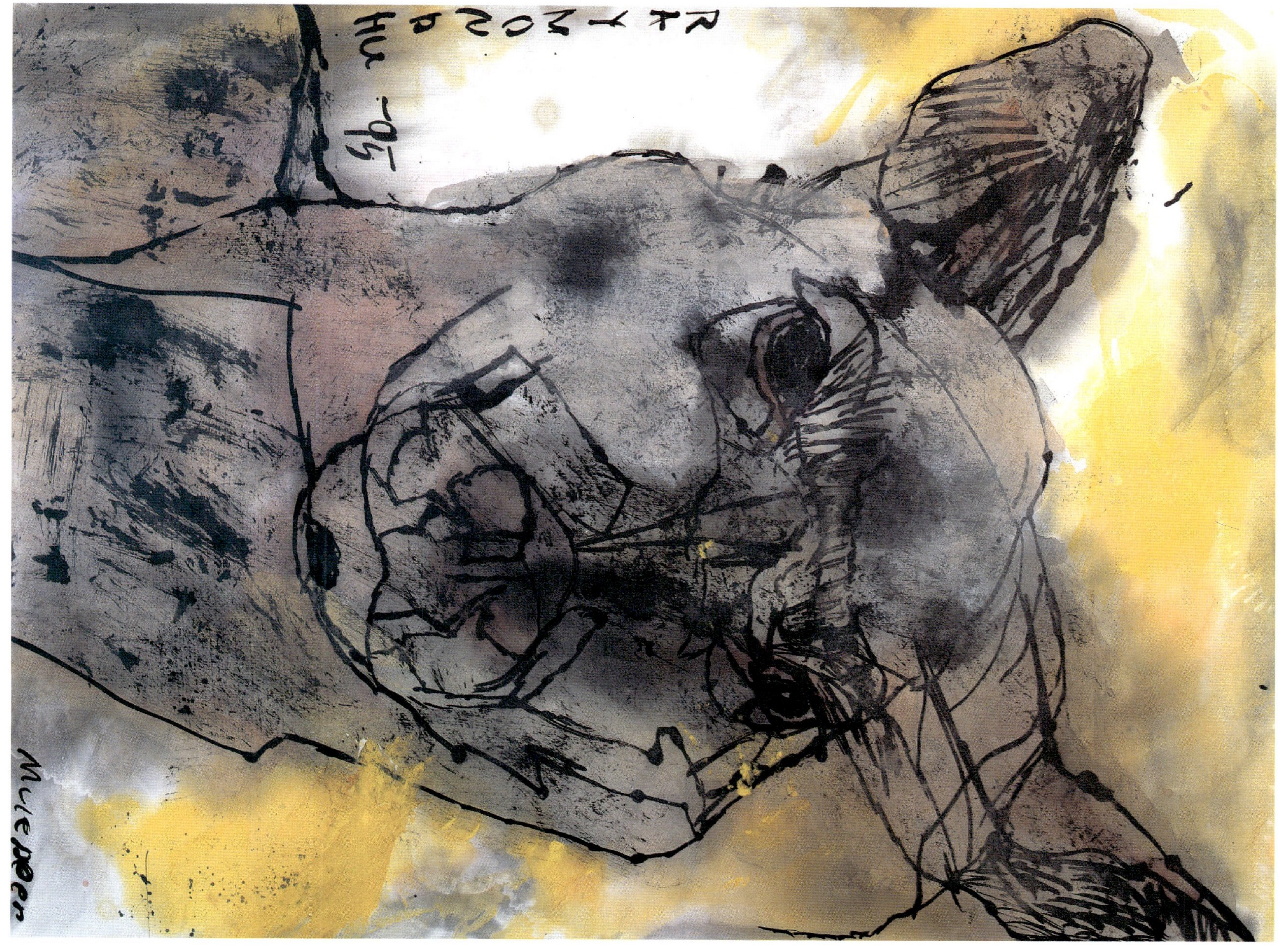

21 • BACK LIT, Chinese Ink & Watercolor on Rice-paper, 18 x 13.5 inches (46 x 34 cm), 1995 　　　彩墨設色紙本 《逆光》

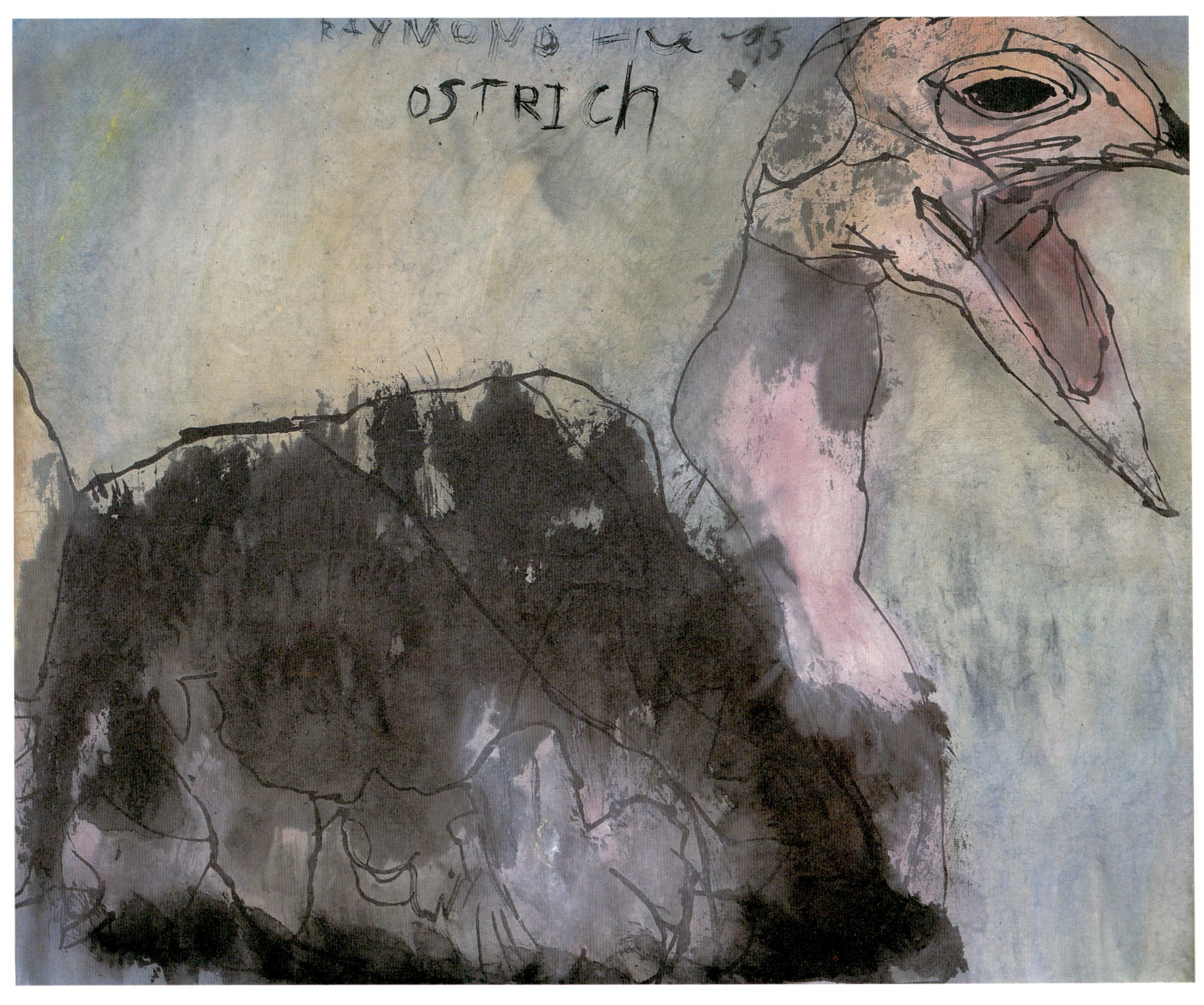

22 • LAUGHING OSTRICH, Chinese Ink & Watercolor on Rice-paper, 16.5 x 20.5 inches (42 x 52 cm), 1995　《歡樂的鴕鳥》

• WHITE DOVE (Detail), Chinese Ink & Watercolor on Rice-paper, 20 x 13.5 inches (51 x 34 cm), 1994　　紙本《和平鴿》

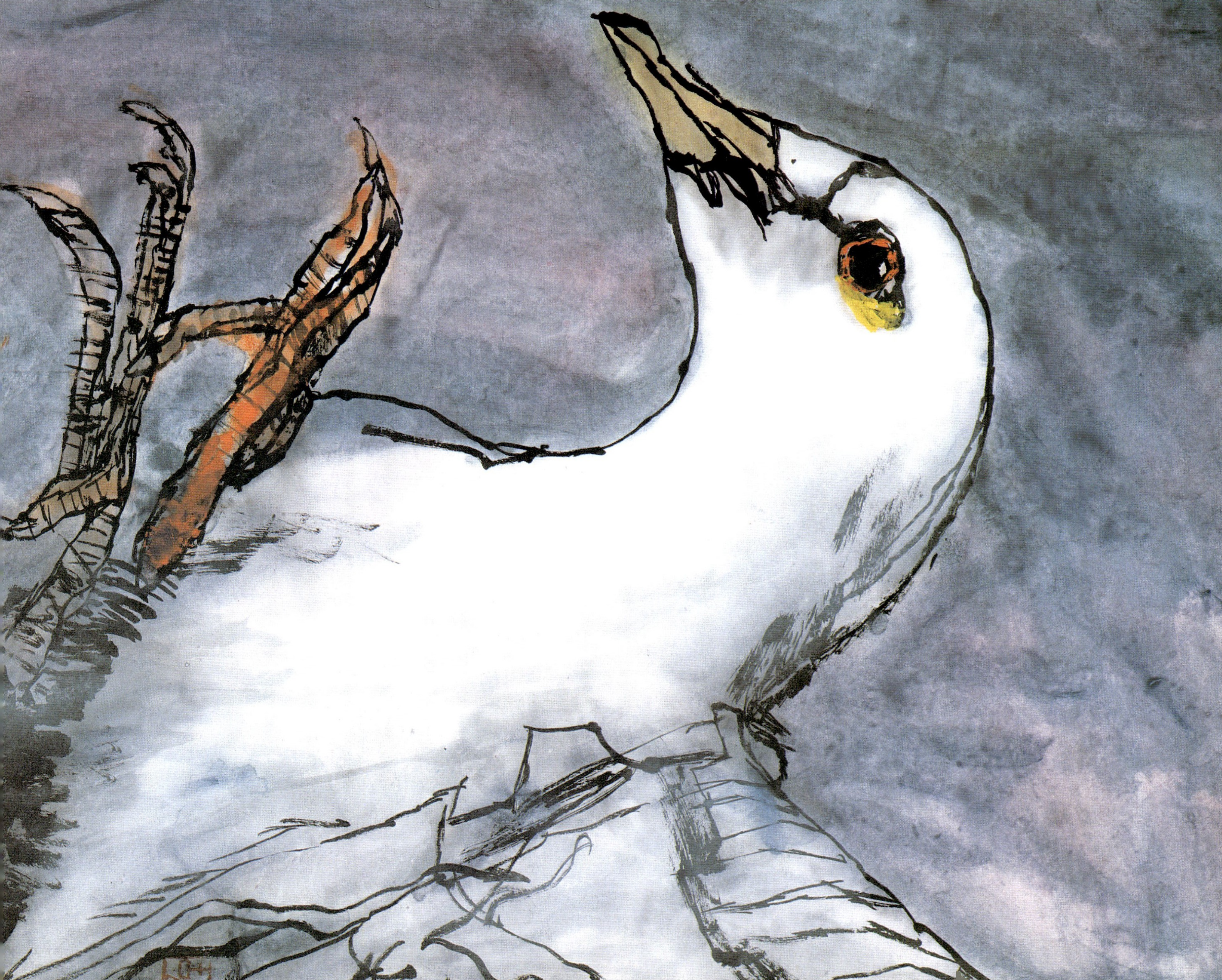

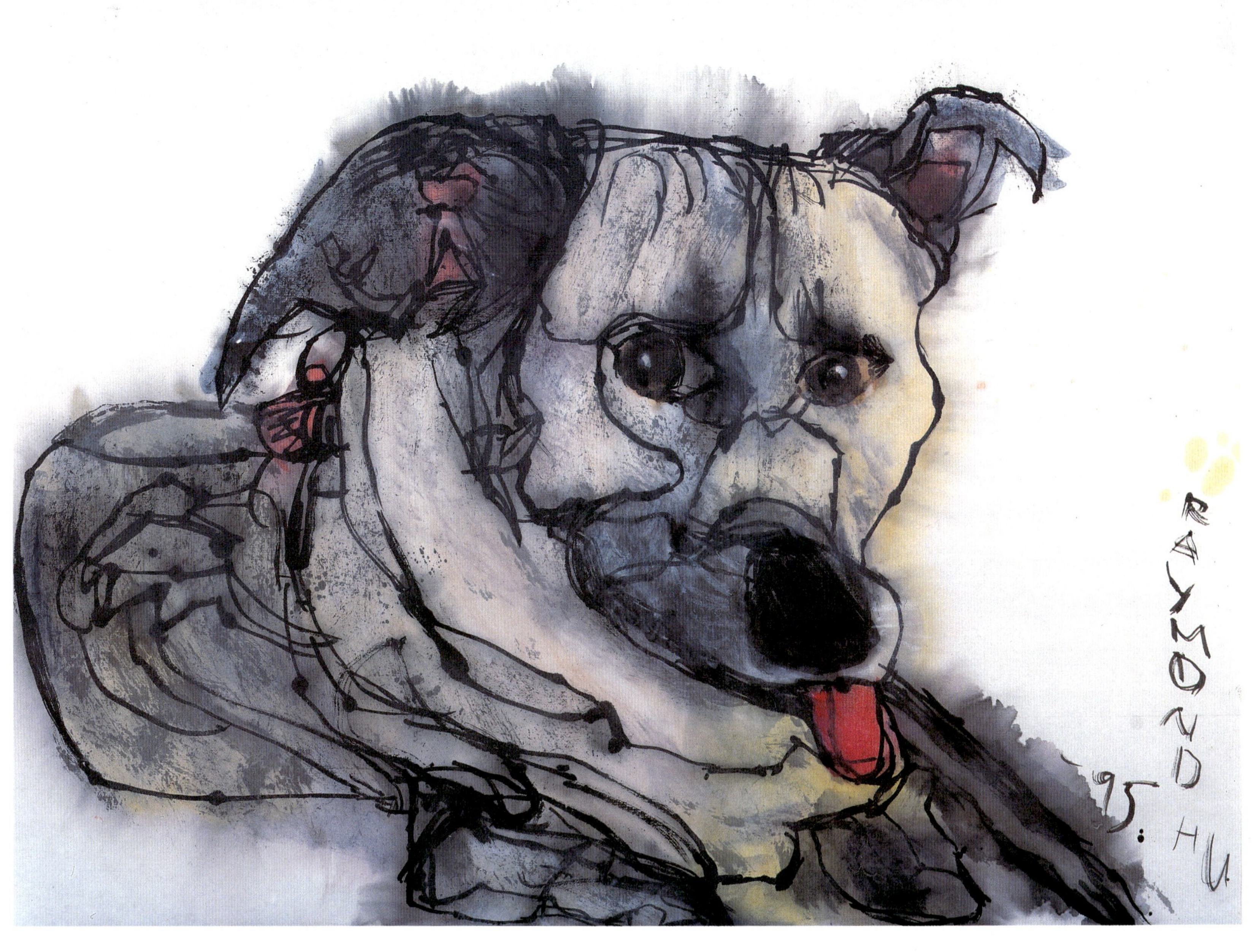

24 • HONEY, Chinese Ink & Watercolor on Rice-paper, 13.5 x 18 inches (34 x 46 cm), 1995　　《可愛的小狗》彩墨設色紙本

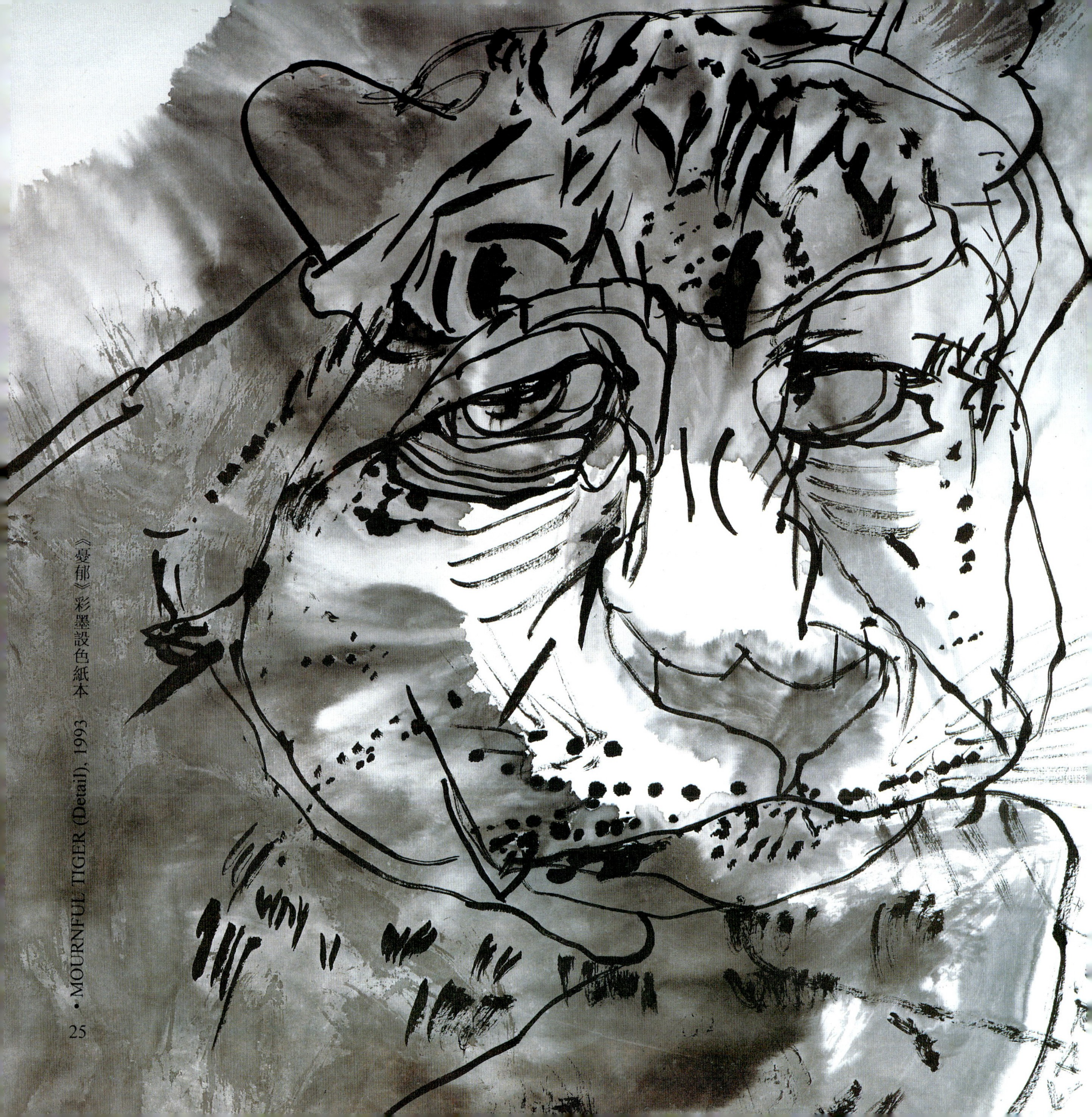

《憂鬱》彩墨設色紙本
• MOURNFUL TIGER (Detail), 1993
25

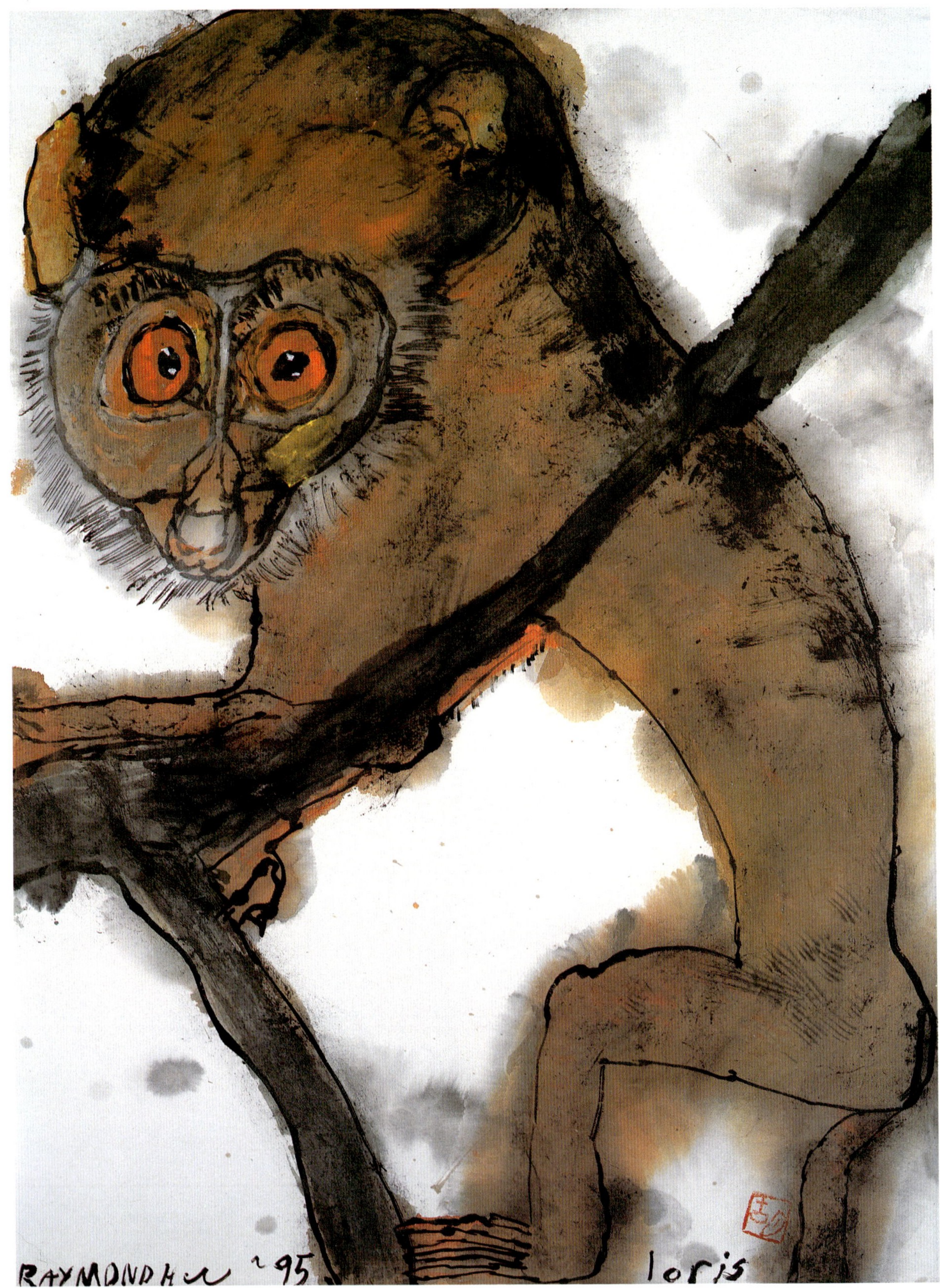

• LORIS, LOOKING BACK, Chinese Ink & Watercolor on Rice-paper, 18 x 13.5 inches (46 x 34 cm), 1995 《回眸》 紙本

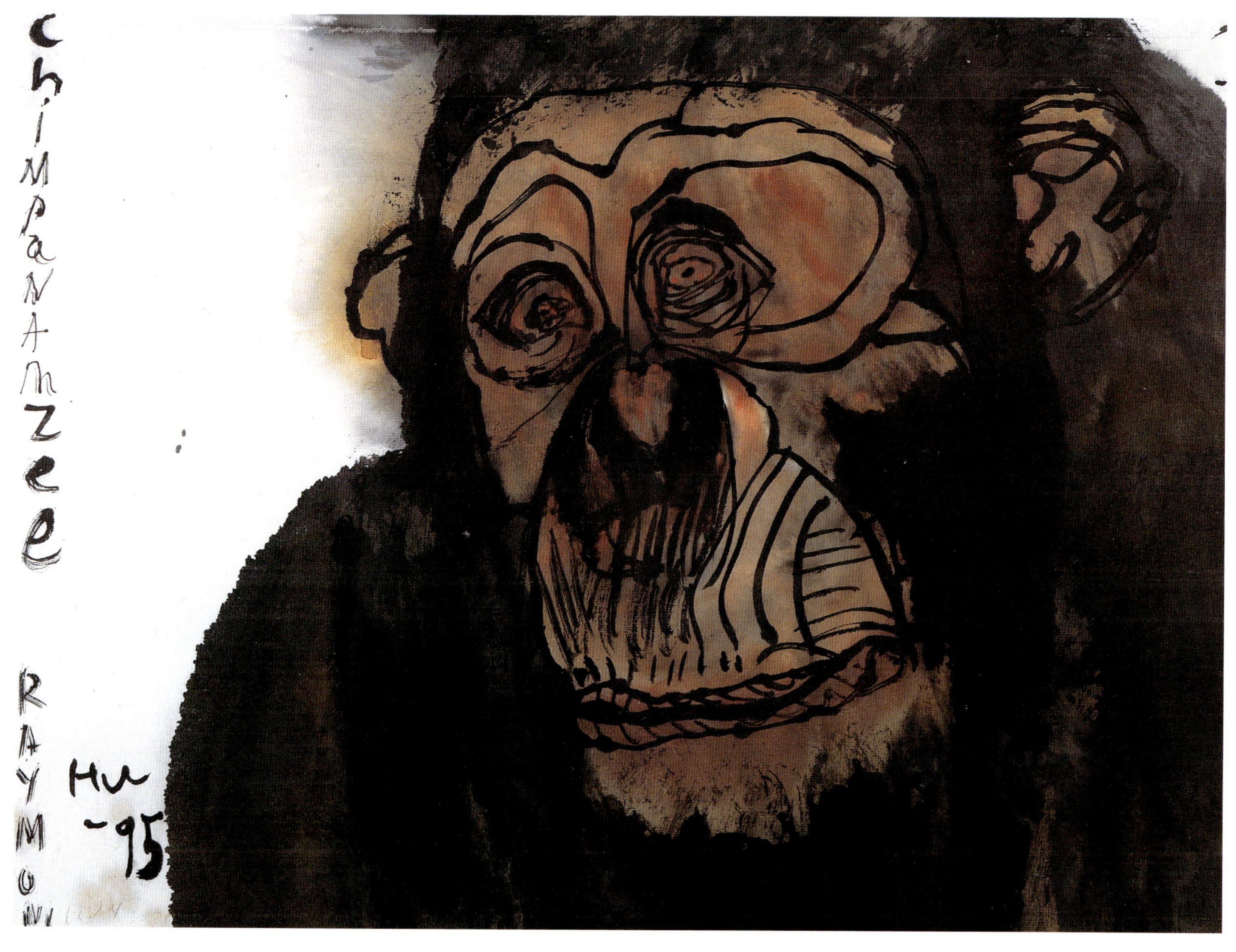

27 • MOODY CHIMPANZEE, Chinese Ink & Watercolor on Rice-paper, 13.5 x 18 inches (34 x 46 cm), 1995 《黑猩猩》 紙本

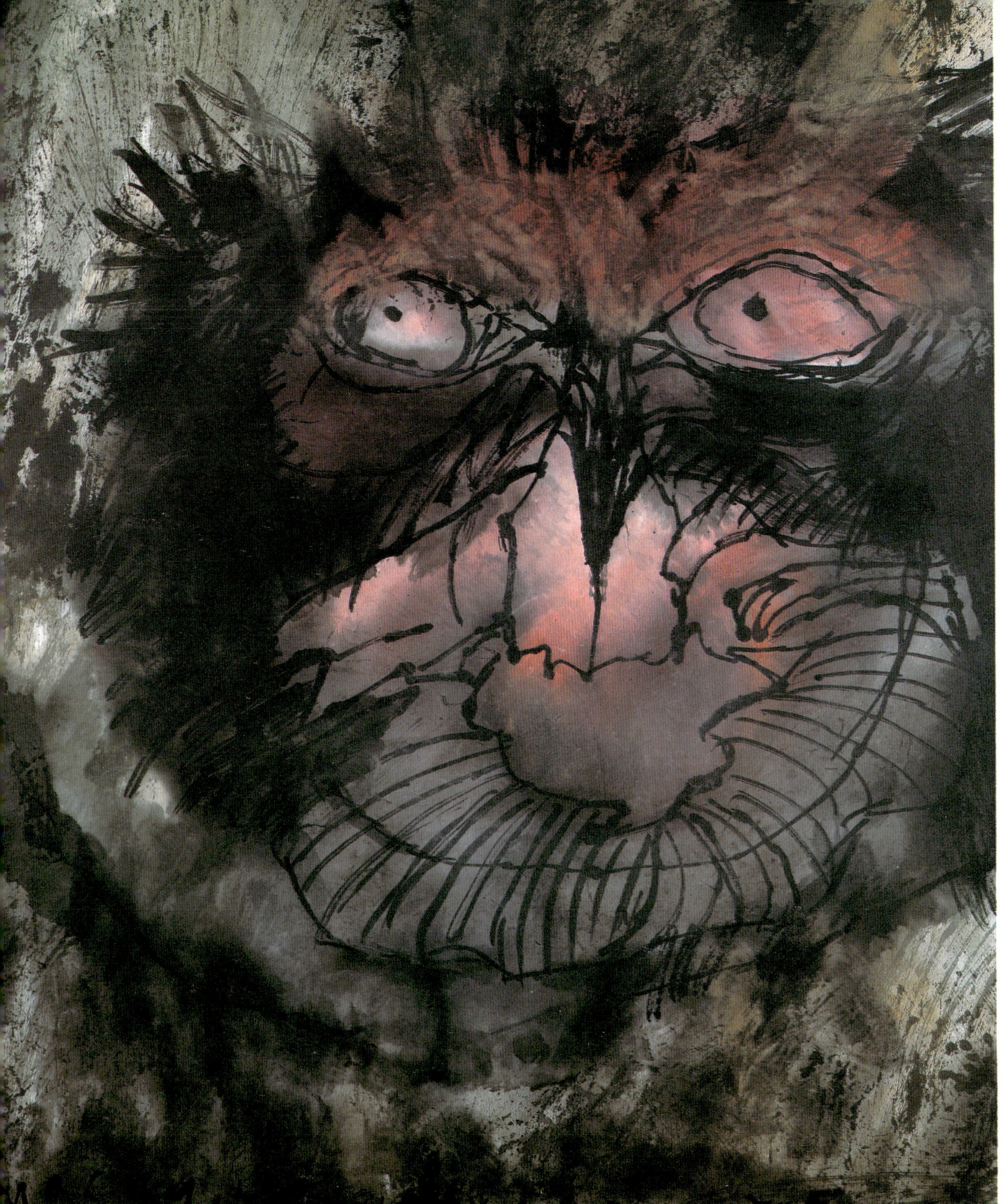

• GLANCING (Detail), Chinese Ink & Watercolor on Rice-paper, 13.5 x 18 inches (34 x 46 cm), 1995

28

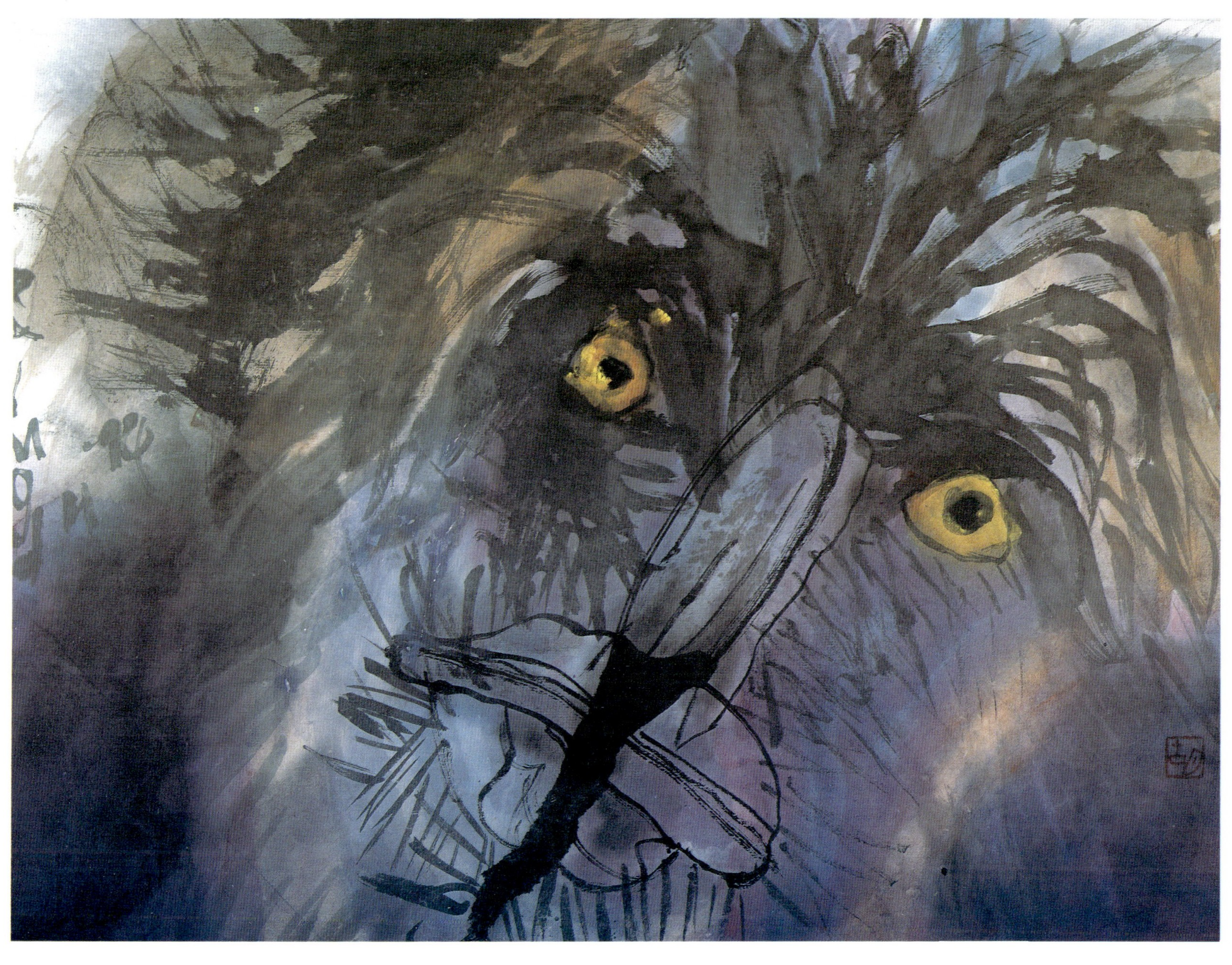

29 • GLOWING EYES, Chinese Ink & Watercolor on Rice-paper, 13.5 x 18 inches (34 x 46 cm), 1994　　《神韻》彩墨設色紙本

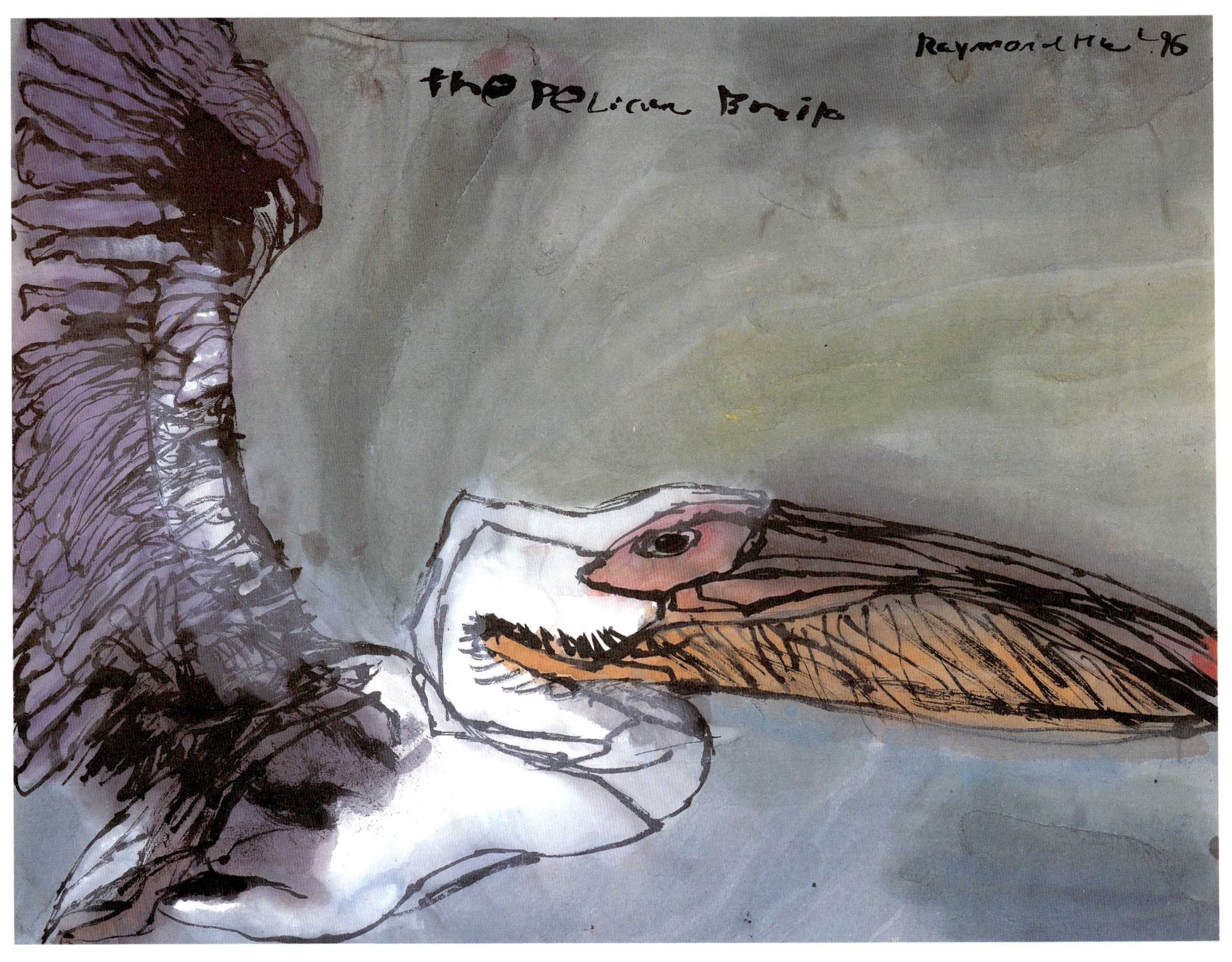

30 • PELICAN IN FLIGHT, Chinese Ink & Watercolor on Rice-paper, 13.5 x 18 inches (34 x 46 cm), 1996 《飛》彩墨設色紙本

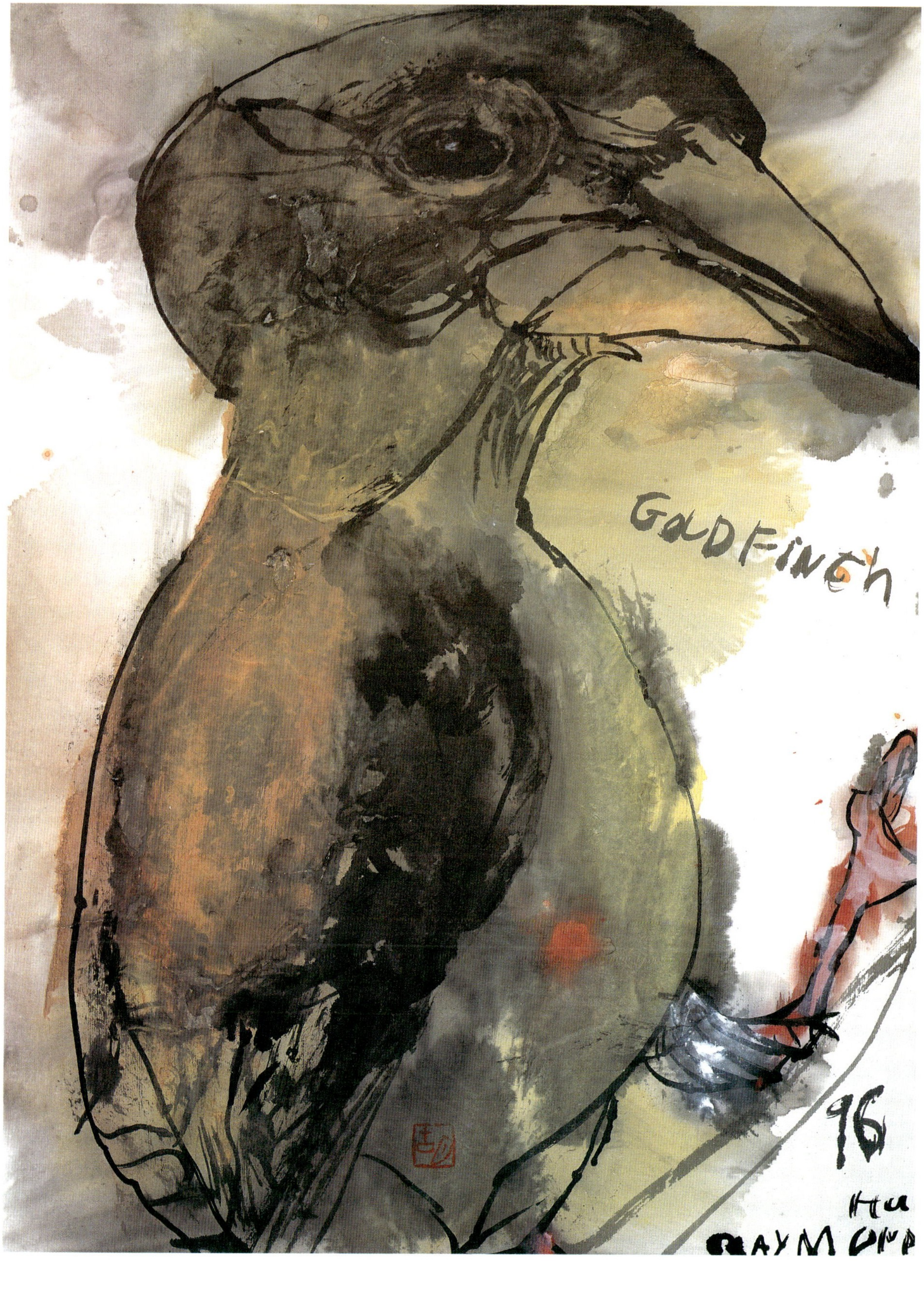

31

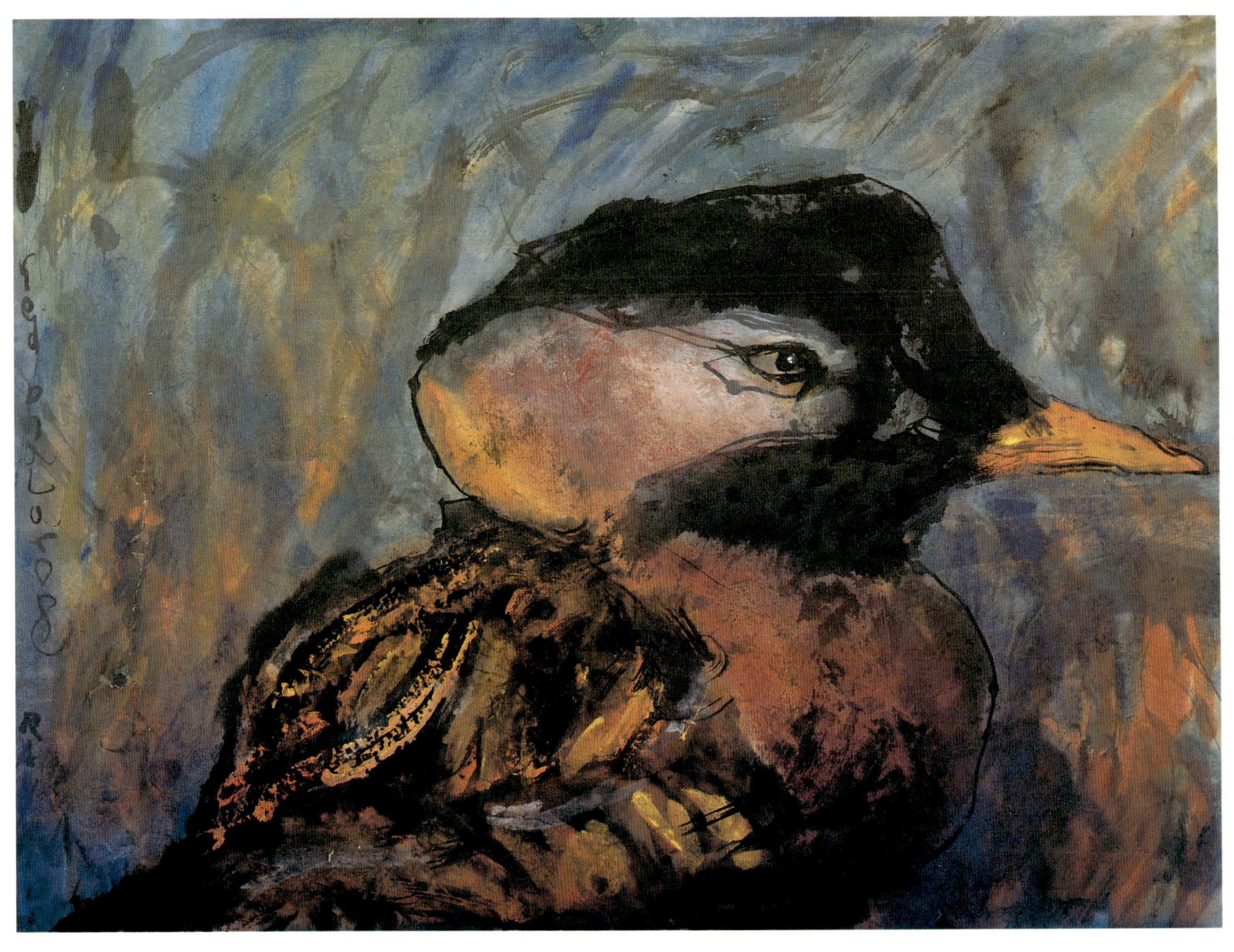

32 • MARSH BY THE BAY, Chinese Ink & Watercolor on Rice-paper, 13.5 x 18 inches (34 x 46 cm), 1996　《湖邊草叢》紙本

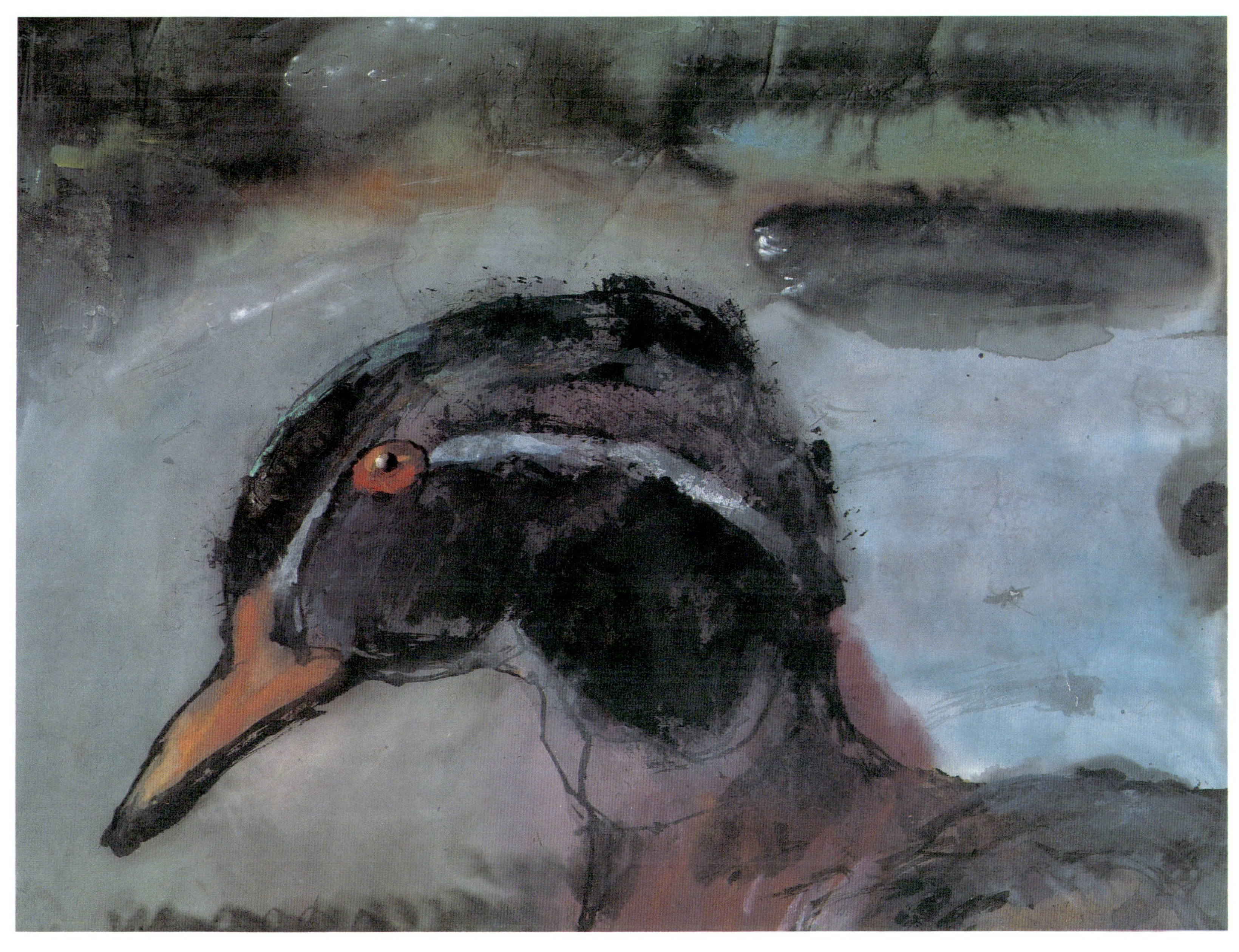

33 • MISTER MALLARD, Chinese Ink & Watercolor on Rice-paper, 13.5 x 18 inches (34 x 46 cm), 1996《悠然》彩墨設色紙本

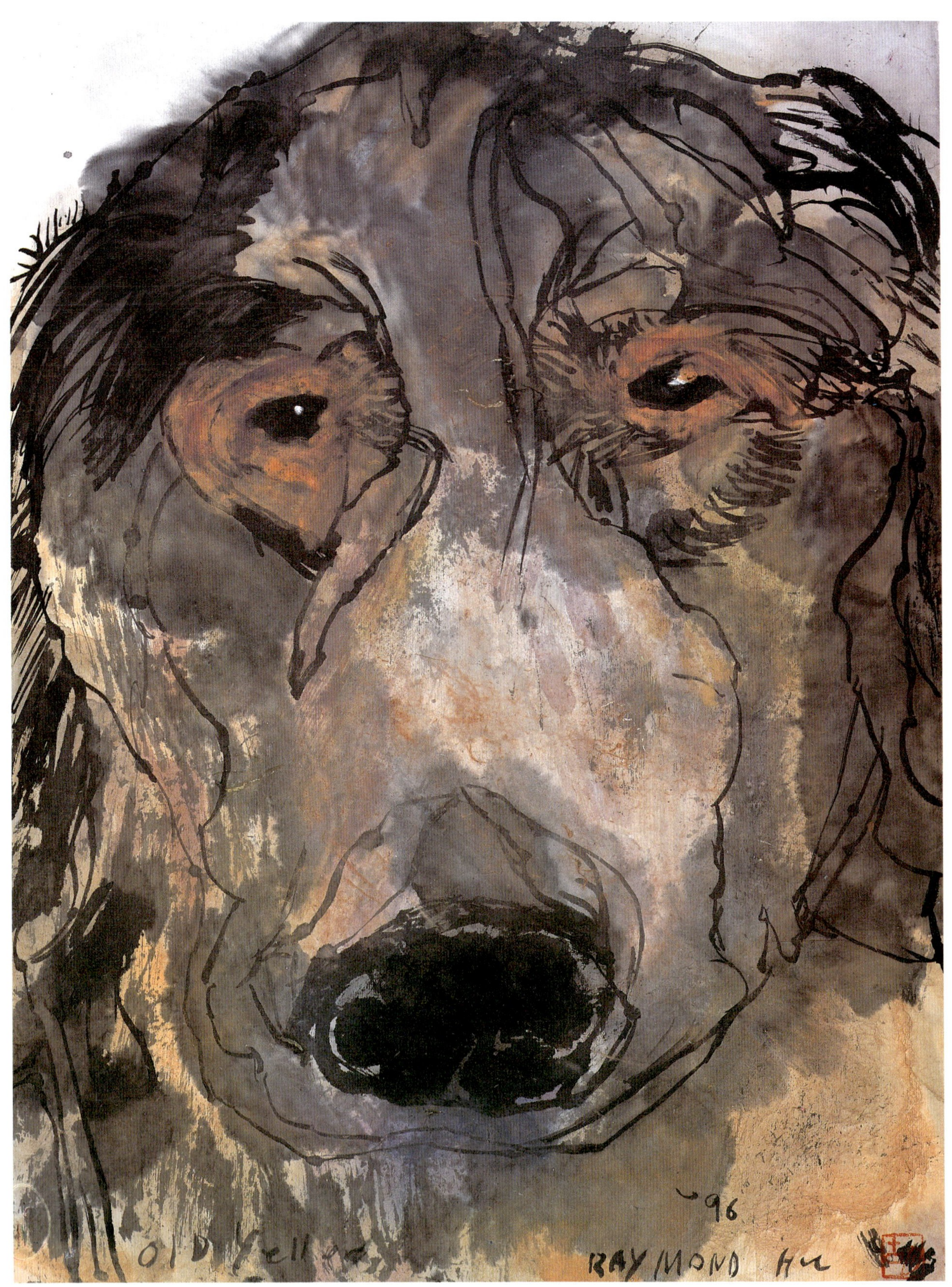

《老君》 彩墨設色紙本

• OLD YELLER, Chinese Ink & Watercolor on Rice-paper, 18 x 13.5 inches (46 x 34 cm), 1996

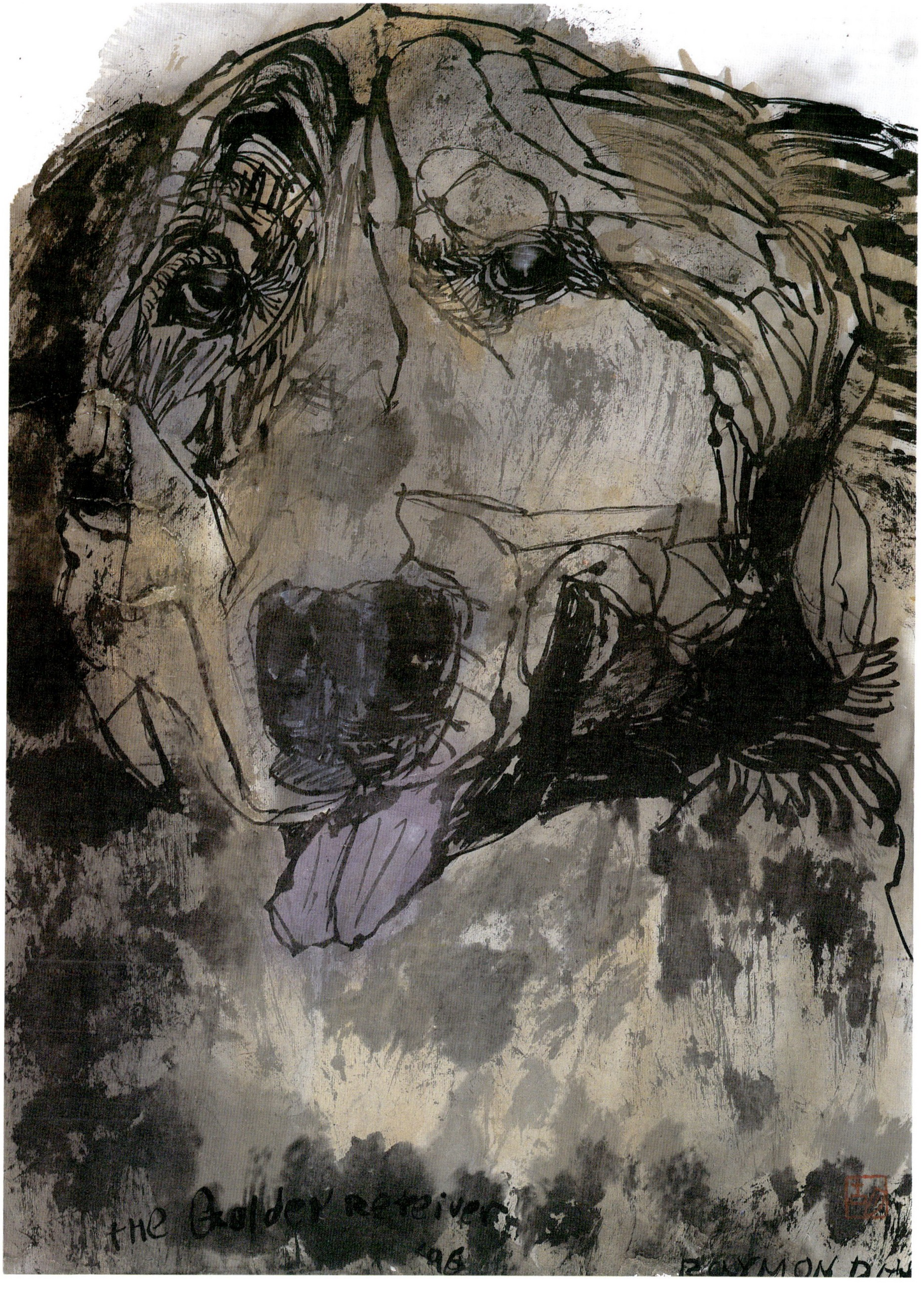

• THE GOLDEN RETRIEVER. Chinese Ink & Watercolor on Rice-paper, 18 x 13.5 inches (46 x 34 cm), 1996　《浩然之氣》

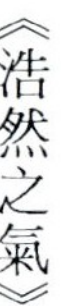

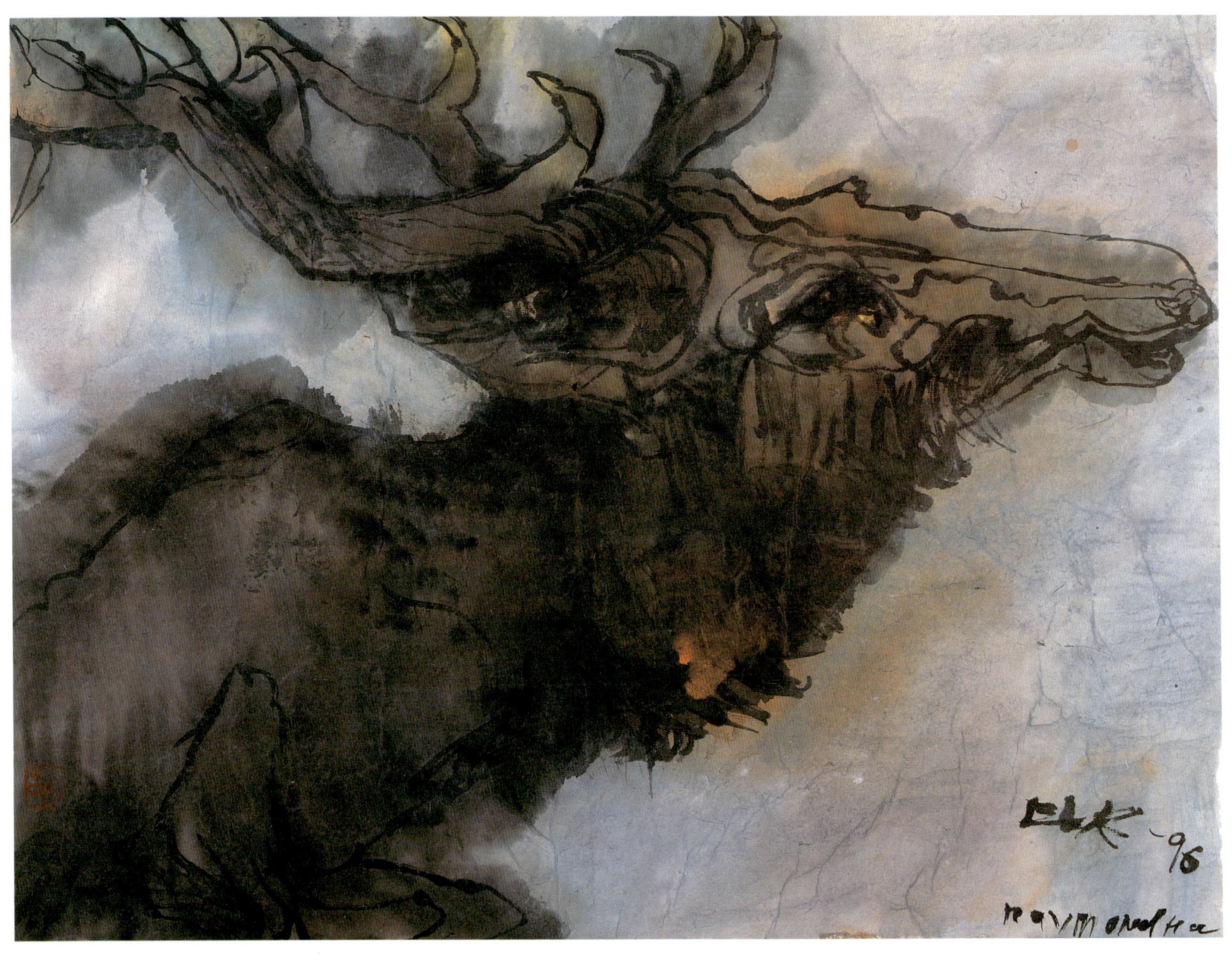

36 • LAKESIDE ELK, Chinese Ink & Watercolor on Rice-paper, 13.5 x 18 inches (34 x 46 cm), 1996 《林邊麋鹿》彩墨設色紙本

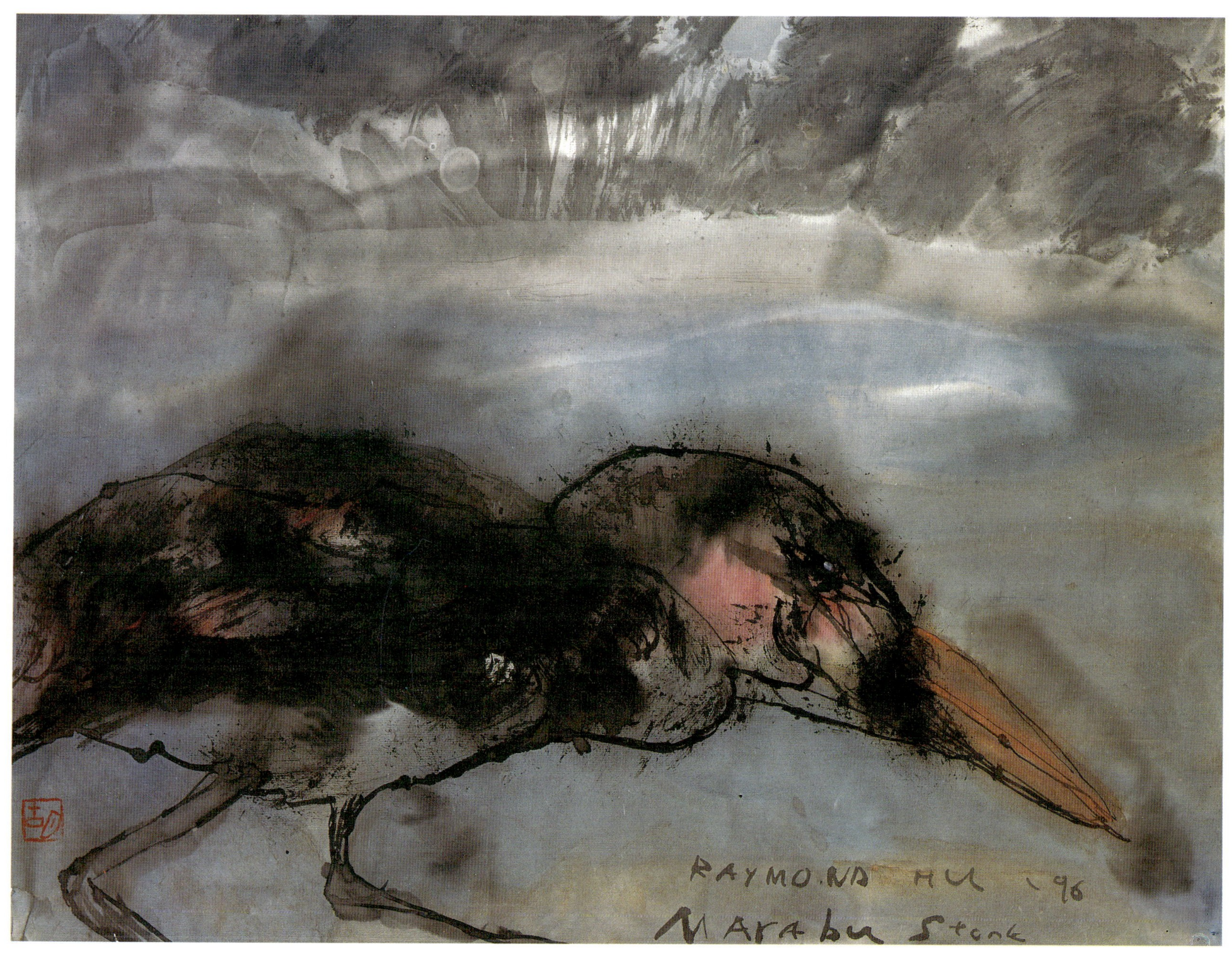

37 • MARABU STORK, Chinese Ink & Watercolor on Rice-paper, 13.5 x 18 inches (34 x 46 cm), 1996《沼澤地》彩墨設色紙本

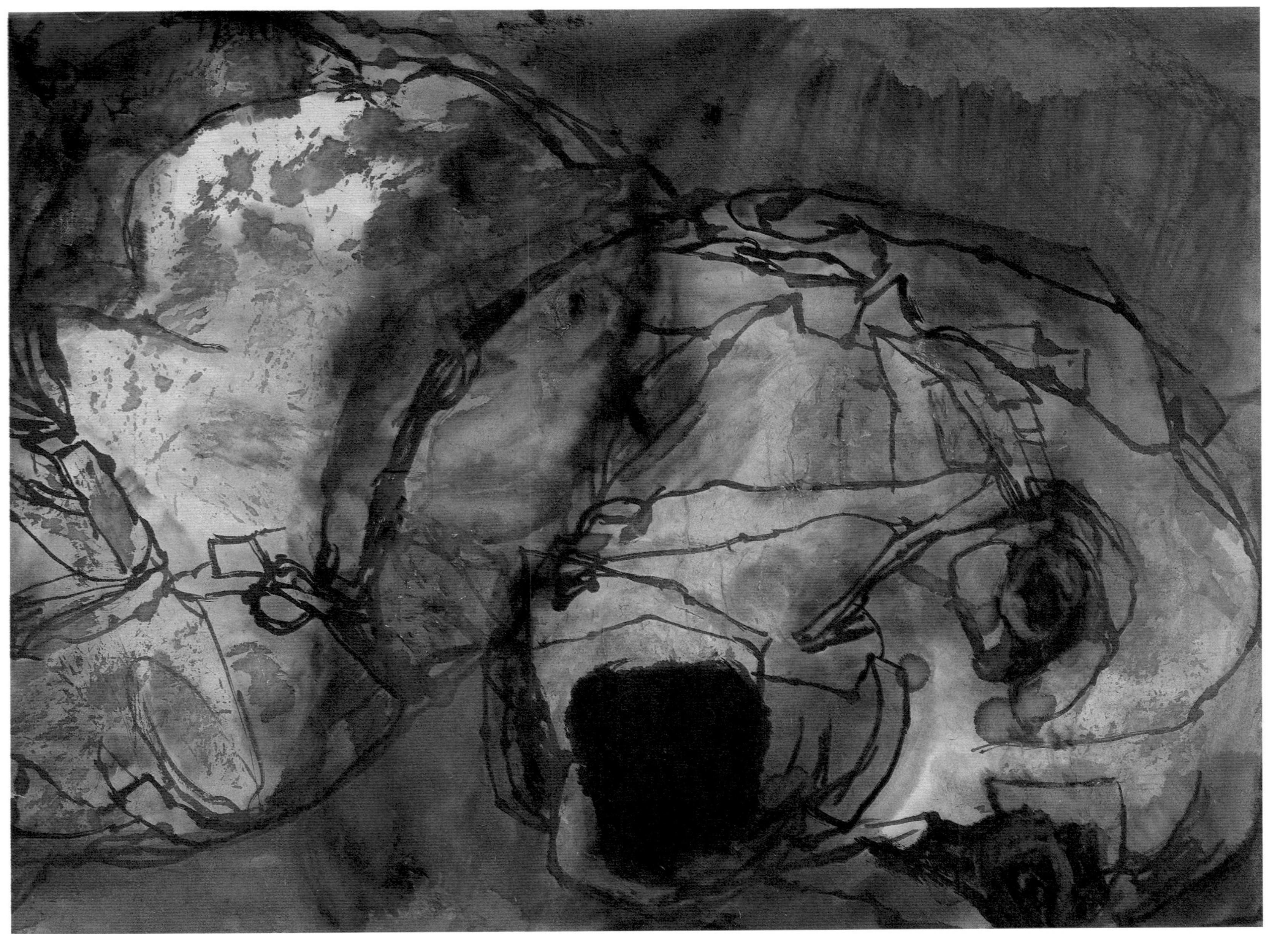

 • BLUE-EYED DALMATIAN, Chinese Ink & Watercolor on Rice-paper, 18 x 13.5 inches (46 x 34 cm), 1996　《藍眼睛》

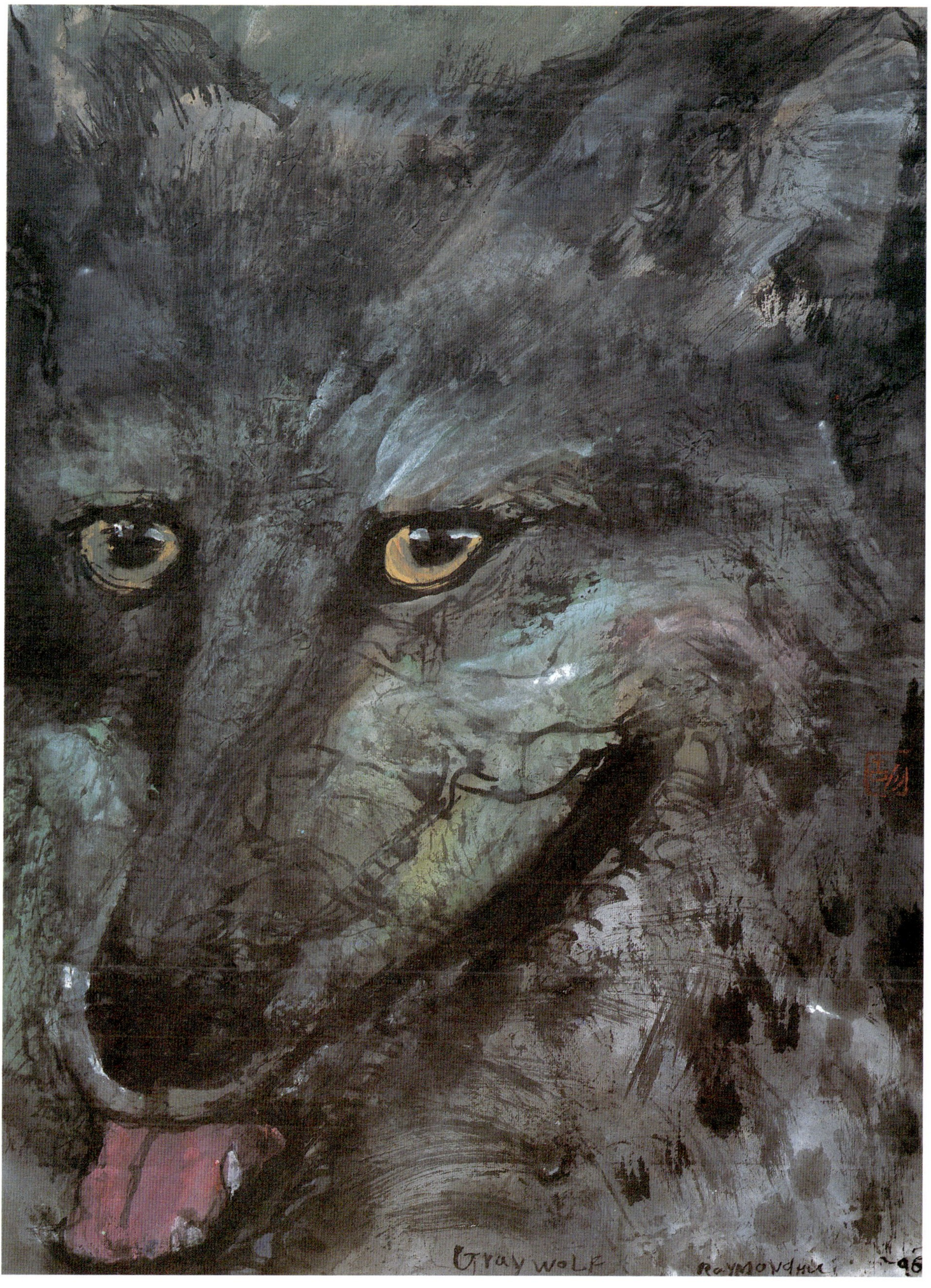

《星夜獵手》 紙本

39 • GRAY WOLF ON THE PROWL, Chinese Ink & Watercolor on Rice-paper, 18 x 13.5 inches. 1996

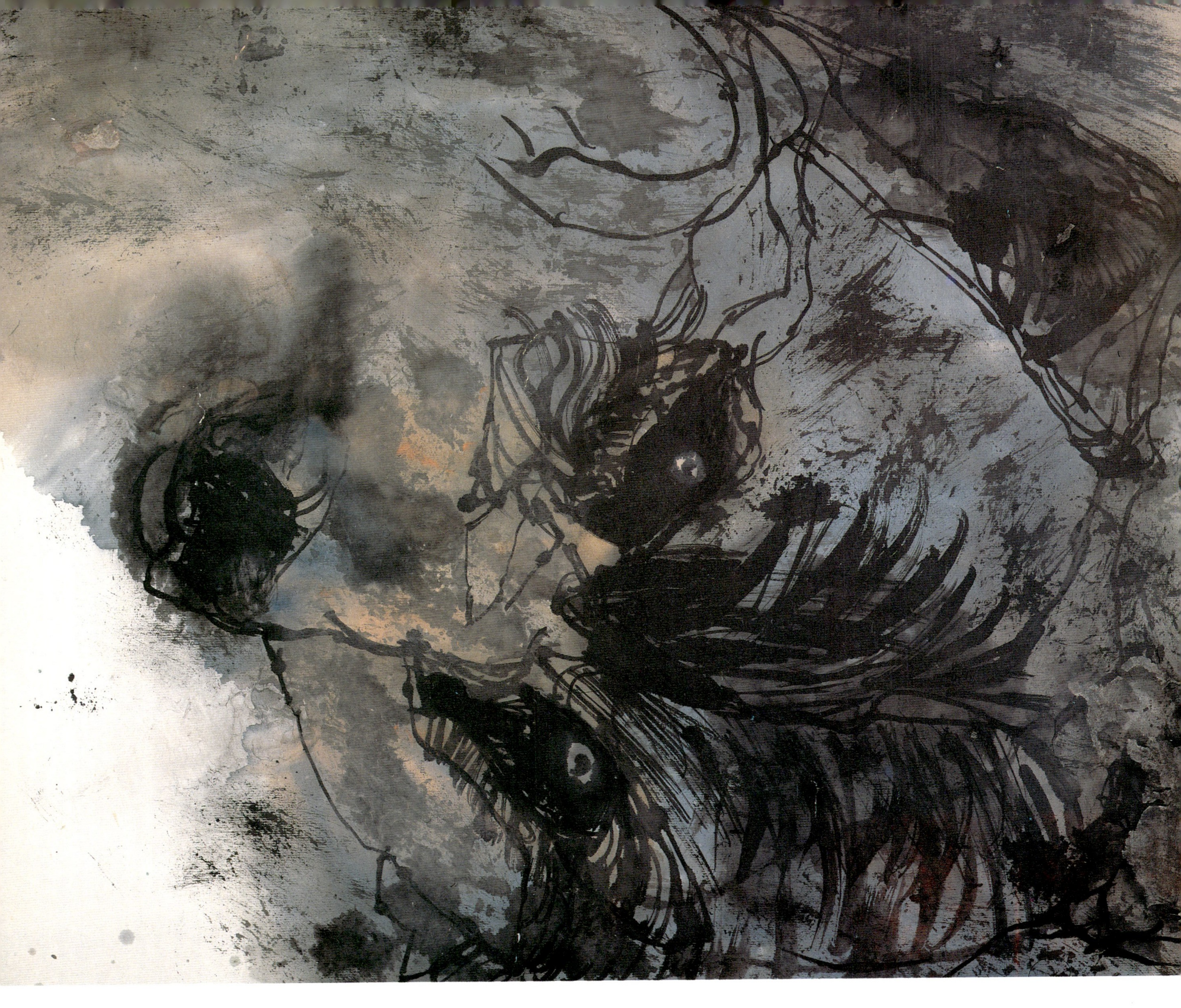

40 • DEEP IN THOUGHT (Detail), Chinese Ink & Watercolor on Rice-paper, 18 x 13.5 inches (46 x 34 cm), 1996 紙本《沉思》

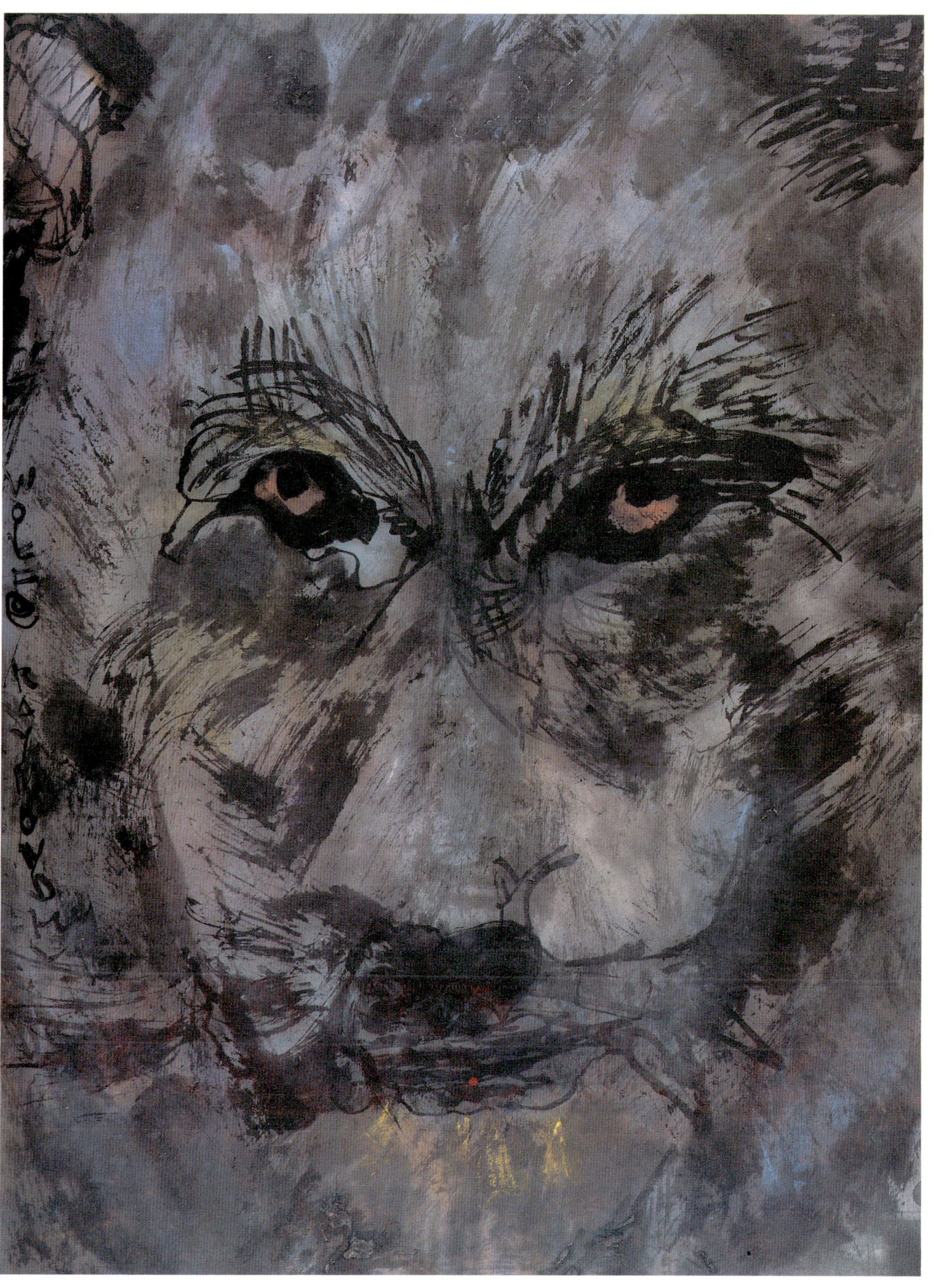

• SOULFUL GAZE, Chinese Ink & Watercolor on Rice-paper, 18 x 13.5 inches (46 x 34 cm), 1996　《瞑想》《瞑想》·彩墨設色紙本

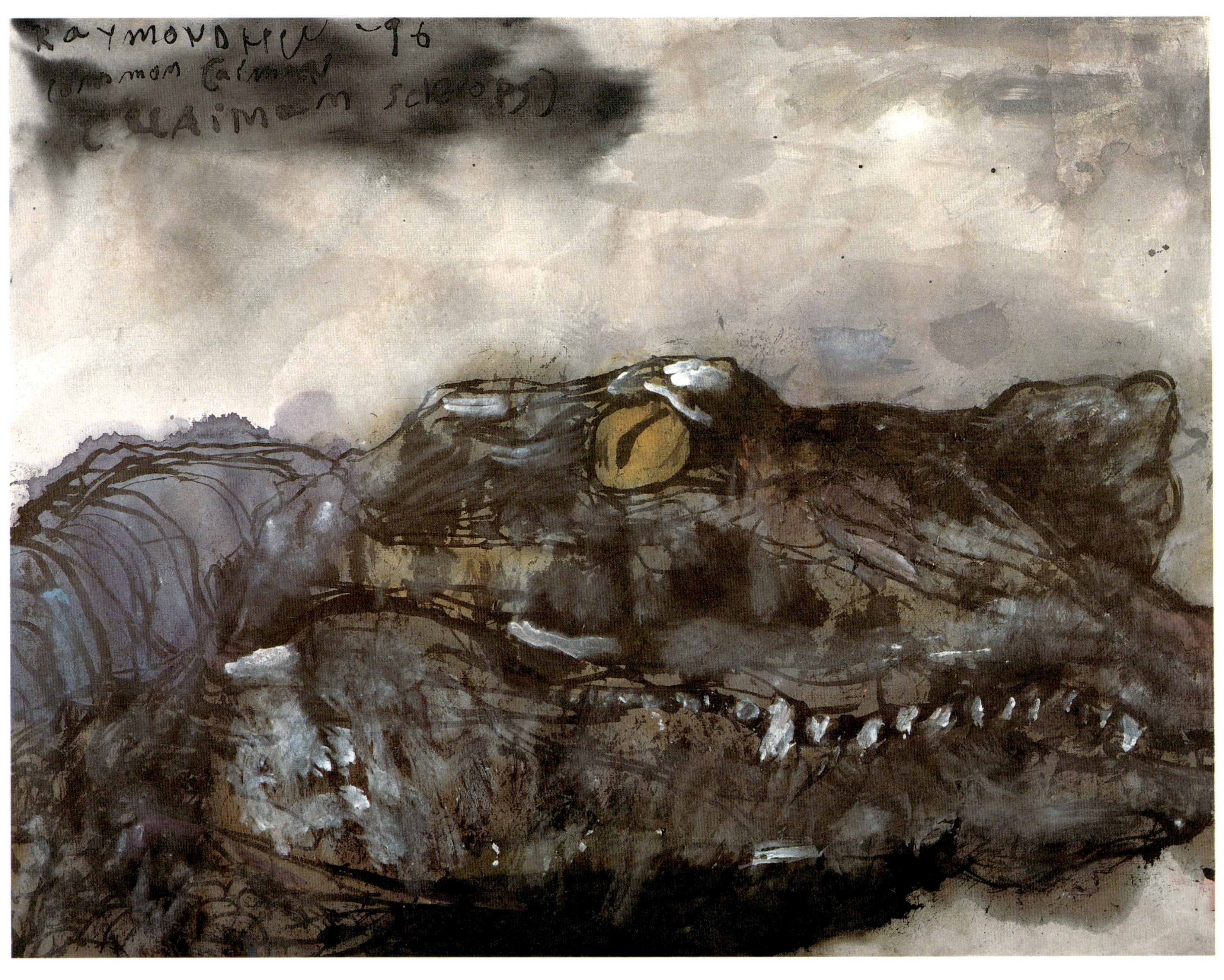

42 • WATCH OUT! Chinese Ink & Watercolor on Rice-paper, 13.5 x 18 inches (34 x 46 cm), 1996 《天邊飄來一朵雲》設色紙本

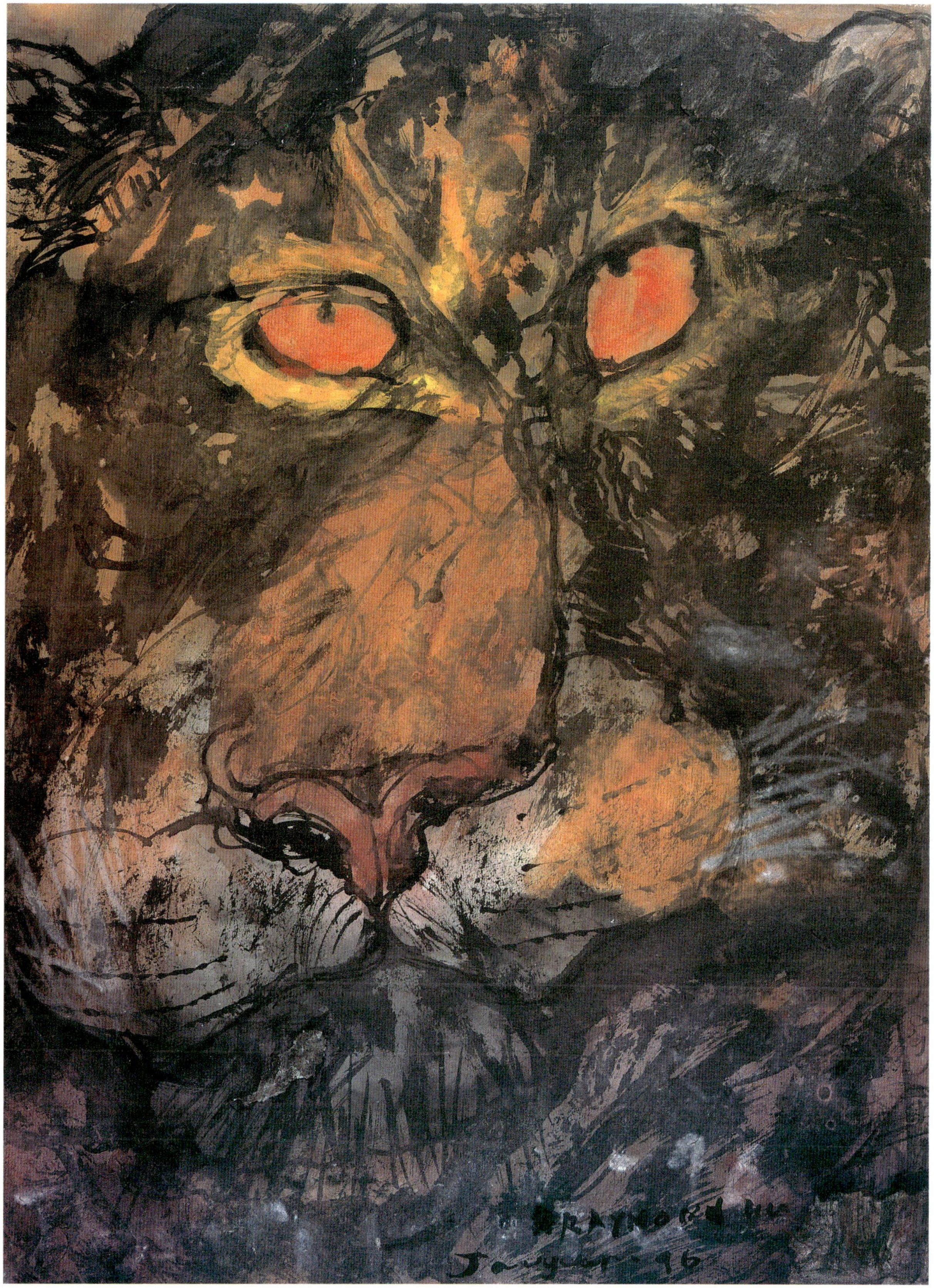

《斜陽》設色紙本

43 • SUNSET IN SUMMER, Chinese Ink & Watercolor on Rice-paper, 18 x 13.5 inches (46 x 34 cm), 1996

BIOGRAPHY OF RAYMOND HU

PERSONAL INFORMATION:

Born on December 10, 1976, Oakland, California, USA,
with Down Syndrome

EDUCATION:

1990-present Study with Chinese brush painting master
    Lampo Leong
1996 Entering Diablo Valley College, Pleasant Hill, CA
1996 Graduated from San Ramon Valley High School,
    Danville, CA

EXHIBITIONS (Selected):

1996 Solo Exhibition, Majorie Evans Gallery, the City
    Gallery of Carmel, Carmel, CA
1996 *California Works*, California Expo., Sacramento, CA
1995 Solo Exhibition, China Art Expo., Guangzhou, China
1995 Solo Exhibit, *Animal Portraits*, Bedford Gallery, Dean
    Lesher Regional Center for the Arts, Walnut Creek
1995 National Down Syndrome Congress, Washington DC
1994 Creative Spirit Gallery, Ghiradelli Square, San
    Francisco, CA (Ongoing)
1994 *Student Art Contest*, California Association for the
    Gifted, Palm Springs, CA (Second Prize)
1993 *A Very Special Art Show*, Sacramento Association for
    the Retarded, Sacramento, CA (*Tiger* won First Prize
    and printed as the 20th anniversary official poster)
1993 *Student Art Competition*, Nanhai Arts Center and
    China Press, Millbrae, CA (Excellence Award)

TELEVISION DOCUMENTARIES & INTERVIEWS:

1996 *Raymond's Portrait*, Documentary of Raymond Hu's
    life and art by Donald Young, KCSM-TV, San Mateo

1996 *Raymond Hu*, Documentary by Cathy Chiang,
    Chinese TV Network, Taiwan (30 min., Chinese)
1995 *Focus,* Interview by Philip Choi, KPST-TV,
    Millbrae, CA (30 min., Chinese)
1995 *Chinese Journal*, Interview by Cathy Chiang,
    KTSF-TV, Brisbane, CA (30 min., Chinese)
1995 *Brush Paintings of Raymond Hu*, by Lampo Leong

BIBLIOGRAPHY (Selected):

———."25 Role Models for the Next 25 Years", *Exceptional
    Parent*, Brookline, MA, 26(6):48, 1996
Leong, Lampo. "Eyes: The Window to the Soul",
    New Evening Post, Hong Kong, Dec. 31, 1995 and
    Santou Evening Post, Guangdong, China, Jan. 14, '96
Baker, Bill. "Tribute to Raymond Hu", US Congressman,
    US Congressional Record, 141(152), Sept. 27, 1995
Nakao, Anne. "Raymond Hu: Painting from the Soul",
    San Francisco Examiner, CA, Oct. 17, 1995
Robinson, Carol. "Disabled Teen Shows Stroke of Genius
    in Art", *San Ramon Valley Times*, Sept. 12, 1995
Fowler, Carol. "Teen's Vibrant Brushwork Brings Animals
    to Life", *Contra Costa Times*, CA, Sept. 12, 1995
He, Yeu-ming. "Animal Paintings of Hu Anyu Received
    Rave Review", *China Press*, Millbrae, Sept. 6, 1995
Dai, Ming-kang. "Hu Anyu, Teenager with Down Syndrome
    Opens Art Show", *World Journal*, Sept. 1, 1995
Linden, Jennifer. "Portrait of the Artist as a Young Man",
    Livery Gazette, CA, Aug. 1994
——— ."Alamo's Raymond Hu's Chinese Brush Art to be
    Displayed at ADAS' Art on the Boardwalk Show",
    Alamo Magazine, Alamo, CA, 8:31, 1994
Sorensen, Andrew. "Teenager Develops Winning Stroke",
    The Sacramento Union, CA, Oct. 6, 1993
Neideffer, Marty. "Student Paints a Bright Busy Future for
    Himself", *TriValley Herald*, CA, March 1, 1993

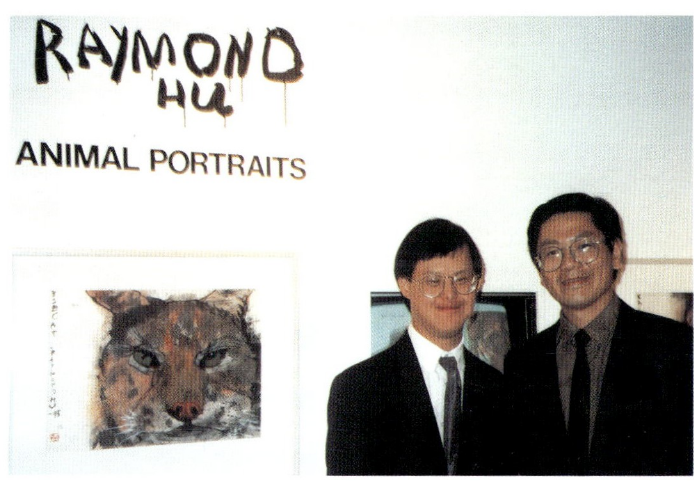

Raymond Hu & Lampo Leong, Walnut Creek Arts Center, 1995

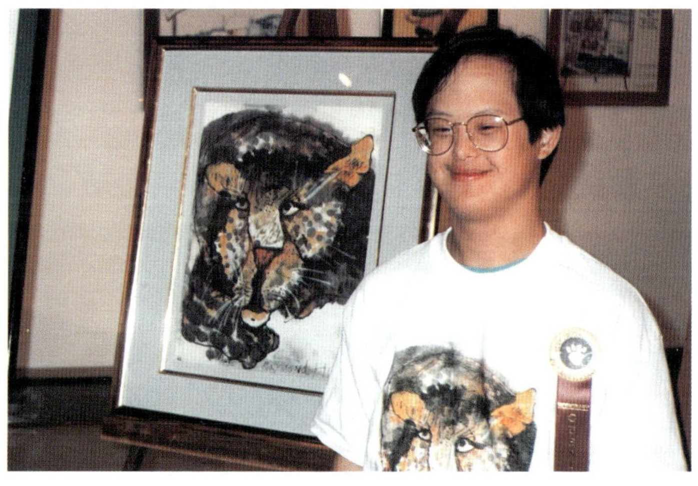

Very Special Art Show, Sacramento, 1993, *Tiger* won First Prize

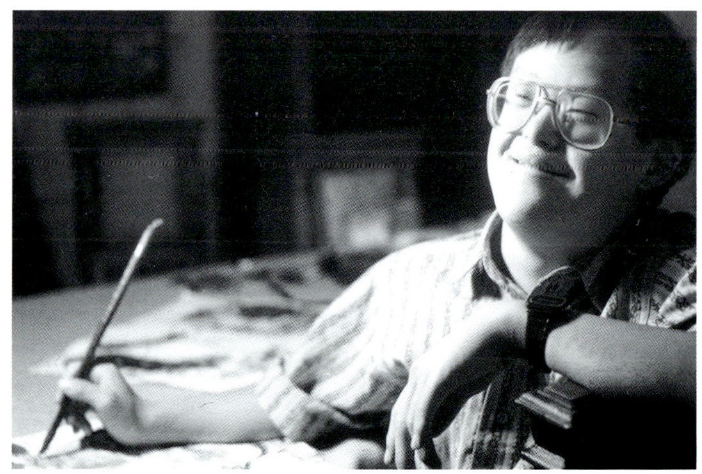

Raymond Hu at work in his painting studio in Alamo, CA, 1993

胡安宇藝術簡歷

1976年12月10日生於美國加州，患有先天性唐氏綜合症
1990年開始師從中國著名畫家梁藍波學習彩墨畫
1996年畢業於美國加州聖雷蒙高中並升入大學

重要畫展及獲獎：

1996年　個人畫展，加州卡邁爾市瑪朱麗·艾文市立畫廊
1996年　加州博覽會《加州美術展》，美國加州沙加緬度市
1995年　個人畫展，中國廣州《中國藝術博覽會》
1995年　個人畫展《動物肖像》，加州核桃溪市藝術中心
1995年　美國華盛頓全國唐氏症年會《美術展覽》
1994年　獲《加州天才學生美術競賽》二等獎
1994年　美國舊金山創意畫廊長期展出
1993年　美國加州首府《特殊美術展》(一等獎·海報)
1993年　獲《第二屆全美中文學校美術競賽》優等獎
1993年　南海藝術中心和《僑報》主辦《兒童美術比賽》優秀獎

主要媒體報導：

1996年　電視記錄片《胡安宇肖像》(45分鐘)，楊文權製作
　　　　　美國加州聖瑪提市　KCSM-TV
1996年　電視記錄片《胡安宇》(30分鐘)，台灣衛星傳訊電視
1996年　"全國25位模範高中生"，華盛頓《傑出父母》雜誌
1996年　"眼睛，靈魂的窗戶"(梁藍波)，香港《新晚報》
1995年　"胡安宇:心靈的畫"，美國《舊金山觀察家報》
1995年　《美國國會記錄》，由美國眾議院貝克議員提出
1995年　電視專訪《焦點·胡安宇》，美國太平洋電視(蔡文耀)
1995年　"殘障少年·美術天才"，美國加州《聖雷蒙時報》
1995年　"華裔少年胡安宇動物畫深得好評"，美國《僑報》
1995年　電視專訪《華人叢刊·胡安宇》，美國KTSF-TV(江瀛)
1995年　"胡安宇舉辦個人畫展"(戴銘康)，美國《世界日報》
1994年　"青年美術家肖像"，美國加州《商事報》
1993年　"少年揮筆獲獎"，美國加州沙加緬度市《聯合報》
1993年　"隻手繪出光明前程"，美國加州《三谷導報》

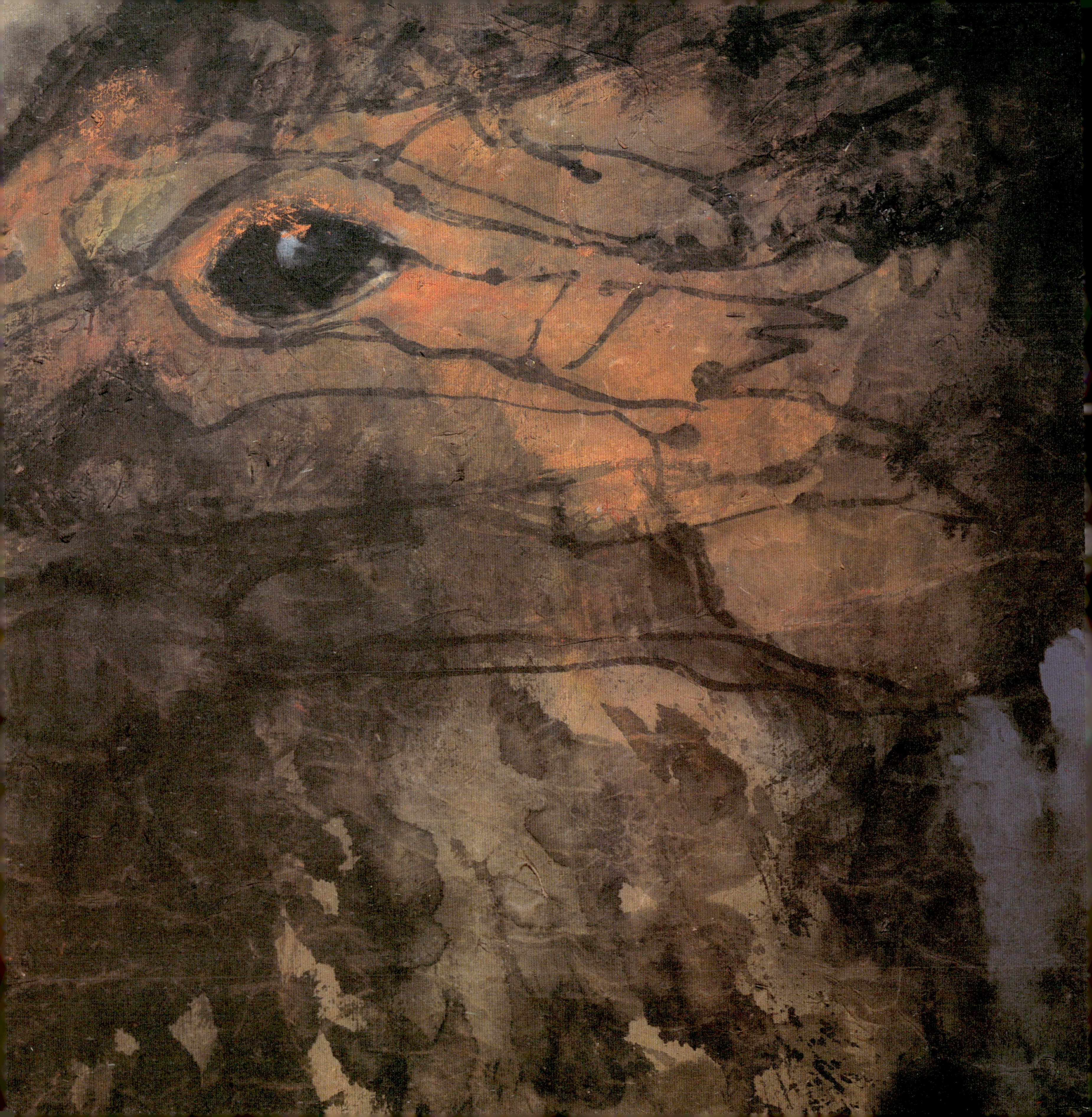

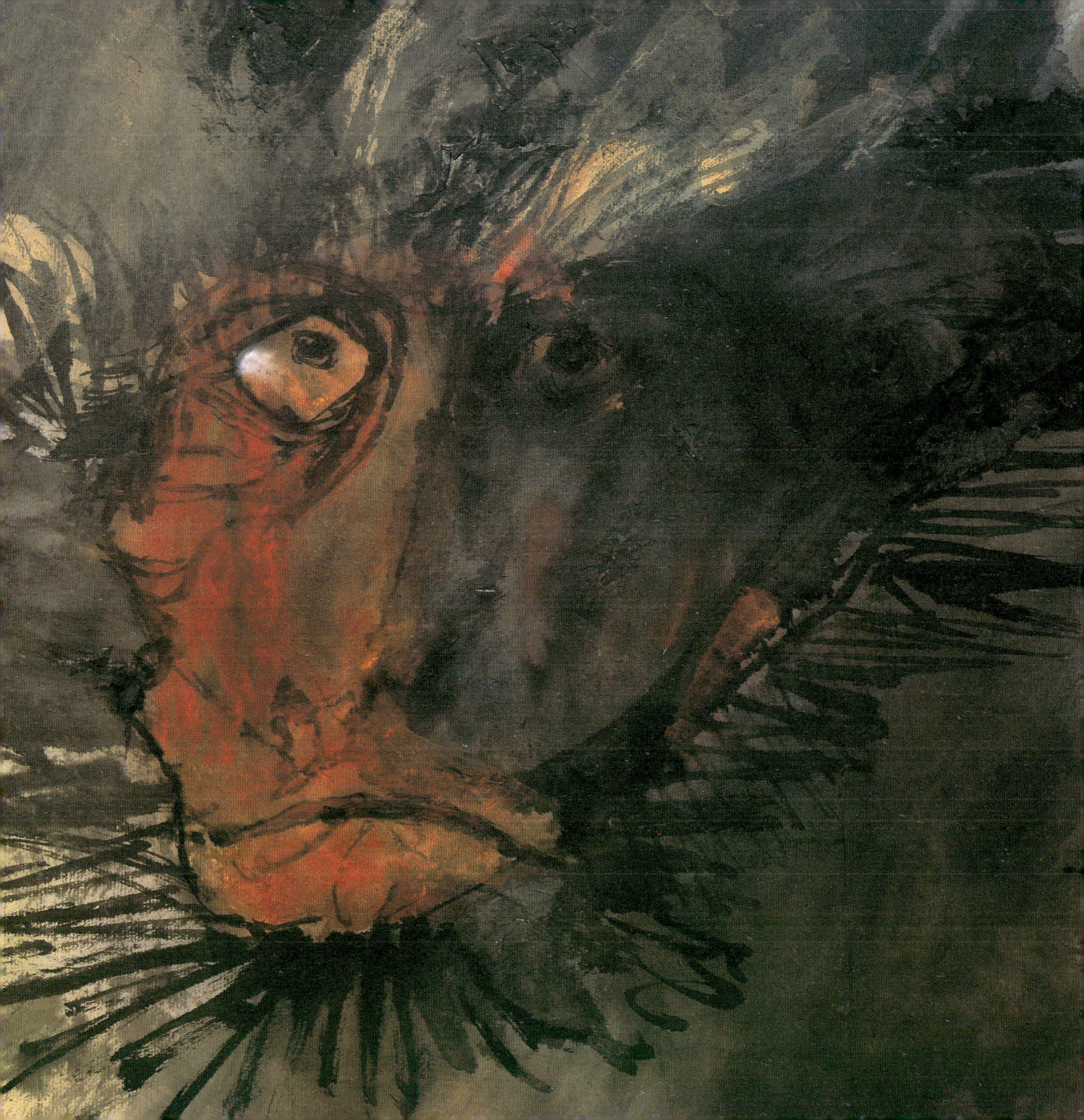

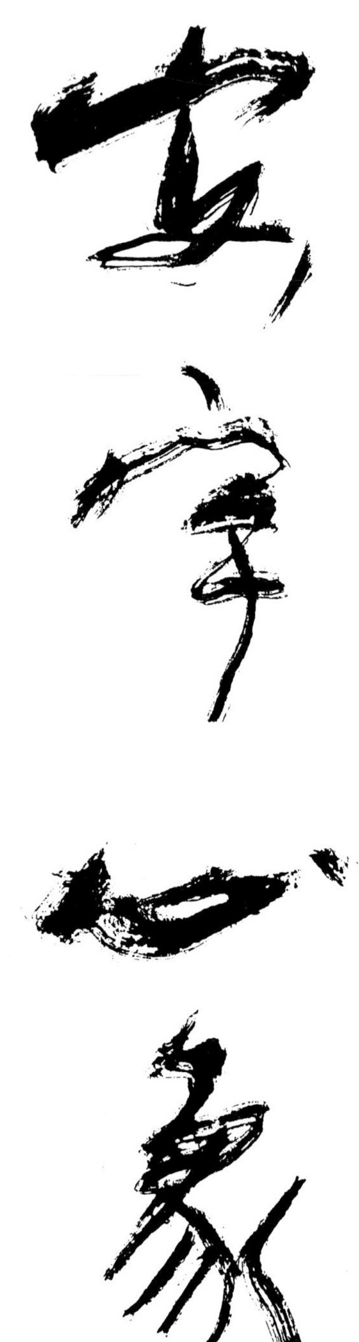